DINING OUT AT HOME
VANCOUVER

Served by
Myriam Leighton & Jennifer Stead
Altitude Publishing

Altitude Publishing Canada Ltd.
1500 Railway Avenue
Canmore, Alberta T1W 1P6
www.altitudepublishing.com
Copyright 2004 © Myriam Leighton and Jennifer Stead

Extreme care has been taken to ensure that all information presented in this book is accurate and up to date, and neither the authors nor the publisher can be held responsible for any errors.

National Library of Canada Cataloguing in Publication

Leighton, Myriam, 1962-
Dining out at home : Vancouver / Myriam Leighton, Jennifer Stead.

Includes index.
ISBN 1-55153-932-2

1. Cookery, International. 2. Restaurants--
British Columbia--Vancouver. I. Stead, Jennifer
II. Title.

TX715.6.L46 2003   641.5'09711'33   C2003-906071-3

Project Development

Cover/illustrations	Jennifer Stead
Cover photo	Doug Leighton
Design/Layout	Scott Manktelow
Editing	Roger McGregor
	Colleen Dorion
	Kara Turner

Altitude GreenTree Program

Altitude Publishing will plant in Canada twice as many trees as were used in the manufacturing of this product.

Made in Western Canada

Printed and bound in Canada by Friesen Printers, Altona, Manitoba

We acknowledge the financial support of the Government of Canada through the Book Publishing Industry Development Program (BPIDP) for our publishing activities.

Table of Contents

Preface

In **Dining Out at Home, Vancouver**, we offer you a selection of recipes from the creative chefs working in the fine restaurants of this city. The diversity of the city of Vancouver is reflected in the variety of the cuisine that you will find in this collection. We hope that it will inspire you and add some excitement to your menus while you are cooking in the comfort of your home.

It has been a wonderful experience working with so many talented chefs, restaurant owners and their administrative staff. When collecting the recipes we have tried to stay true to individual styles and approachs. The result is a melange of meals from a wide range of restaurants sure to satisfy everyone. One consistent interest among all the chefs is their appreciation for their environment and an unbounding love of all that is wonderful about the West Coast. Most take advantage of the opportunity their city affords them to use local, often organic, ingredients including fresh fish, seafood, fruits, vegetables and herbs.

We would like to thank and acknowledge all the exceptional restaurants and chefs for their time and creative generosity, our food editors, Colleen Dorion and Roger McGregor, and all the other people who made this book possible.

Bon appetite!

Myriam and Jennifer

Bonus! Recipe Sampler!

Additional recipes are available on the web.
Please visit **www.altitudepublishing.com**
and follow the links to
Dining Out at Home, Vancouver.

Appetizers, Sauces & Sides

Seared Ahi Tuna and Duck Confit Terrine
with Plum Sake Gelée

Serves: 4

Confit Duck Legs

2	Duck legs	2
2	Oranges, zest	2
4 cups	Duck fat or olive oil	1 litre
1 tbsp.	Flat leaf parsley, finely chopped	15 ml
to taste	Salt and pepper	to taste
1/4 cup	Butter, clarified	50 ml

In a medium size saucepan on low heat, brown duck legs, skin side down until golden brown for approximately 5 minutes. Turn legs over and slowly add duck fat and orange zest. Bring oil to a low simmer, remove from heat and cover pot with lid. Place in preheated 250°F (120°C) oven and cook until duck legs are tender — approximately 2 hours. When duck is cooked, remove from oven and let legs cool in oil. When cool enough to handle, pick meat off the bone into a clean container. Add parsley, salt and pepper. Set aside.

Ahi Tuna

1 lb.	Ahi tuna	450 g
1 1/2 tsp.	Salt	7 ml
1 1/2 tsp.	Black pepper	7 ml

Ask your butcher to cut the fresh tuna, 6 inches (15 cm) long, 1 1/2 inches (4 cm) wide and 2 inches (5 cm) thick.

Season tuna generously with salt and black pepper. Heat a non-stick frying pan over high heat until almost smoking and quickly sear tuna on all four sides so centre is still rare and cool to touch. When tuna is cool, carefully cut lengthwise into 2 pieces, then once again to make 4 pieces in total, each 6 inches (15 cm) long.

Assembly: Line terrine mould with plastic wrap and place one piece of tuna in bottom with seared side down. Brush with clarified butter. Gently press 1/3 of the duck confit mixture on top of the tuna and brush again with butter. Repeat process until last piece of tuna is on top with seared side up. Fold plastic wrap over top, place 2 lbs. (1 kg) of weight on top and refrigerate overnight.

Plum Sake Gelée

1 cup	Plum juice	250 ml
1/2 cup	Plum sake wine	125 ml
3 leaves	Gelatin soaked in cold water	3 leaves

Combine juice and wine in a heavy saucepan and reduce by half. Remove from heat. Add strained gelatin to reduction and dissolve for 10 minutes. Cover and chill in the refrigerator for 3 hours.

To serve: Lift terrine from mould and slice off 1/4 inch (6 mm) pieces. Plate 3 slices of terrine with a micro green salad and garnish with Plum Sake Gelée.

Wine suggestion: Tinhorn Creek Winery, Gewurztraminer, Okanagan Valley, 2002

Scott Baechler, Executive Chef
Diva at the Met

Radicchio Bocconcini

Serves: 4

12	Small bocconcini (fresh mozzarella), cut in half	12
2 tbsp.	Olive oil, extra virgin	30 ml
1 tsp.	Fresh thyme	5 ml
2 tbsp.	Fresh basil	30 ml
1 tbsp.	Fresh oregano	15 ml
1 tbsp.	Paprika, powder	15 ml
to taste	Salt and pepper	to taste
6 slices	Parma prosciutto	6 slices
12	Large radicchio leaves, wilted	12
1/2 cup	Sour cherry syrup	125 ml
1/2 cup	Red wine vinegar	125 ml

Marinate bocconcini overnight in olive oil, fresh herbs, paprika, salt and pepper.

Wrap prosciutto around marinated bocconcini. Roll prosciutto and bocconcini in bundles in wilted raddicchio leaves. Add sour cherry syrup and red wine vinegar to a sauté pan and reduce by one half over medium-high heat.

Grill raddicchio bundles over medium-high heat until cheese starts to soften. Remove from grill and place in the cherry vinaigrette.

Chef's tip: Give the raddicchio bundles a squeeze, gently breaking the raddicchio spine. This keeps the bundles tight during grilling.

Serving suggestion: Serve warm on a bed of greens or endive leaves

Robert Parrott, Executive Chef
Gusto di Quattro

Tartare of Ahi Tuna, Scallops and Oysters

Serves: 1

1/2 oz.	Tuna	15 g
1/2 oz.	Scallops	15 g
2	Beach oysters	2
1/2 tbsp.	Chives, chopped	7 ml
1 tsp.	Shallots, chopped	5 ml
1/2 tbsp.	Lime juice	7 ml
1 tbsp.	Lobster oil	15 ml
	(available from The Cannery)	
to taste	Salt and pepper	to taste
3 pcs.	Nori seaweed	3 pcs.

Cut all fish into small 1/8 inch (3 mm) cubes. Add chopped chives, shallots, lime juice and oil. Mix well over an iced bowl, add seasoning and let sit.

To deep fry nori seaweed, cut into desired shape. Put under water for 2 seconds and put into deep fryer at 300°F (150°C). Be very careful as water may cause oil to spit. Cook for 1 minute and turn over. Remove from deep fryer and place on a clean paper towel to absorb excess oil. Reserve and use as a base for tartare.

Soya and Wasabi Sauce

1/3 cup	Soya sauce	75 ml
1/2 tsp.	Honey	2 ml
1/2 tsp.	Wasabi powder	2 ml

Mix soya sauce with honey. Put the dried wasabi mustard in a bowl then add the soya sauce and honey and mix together.

To serve: Place a sheet of nori seaweed on a plate with some triangles of toast. Add the fish tartare and serve with soya and wasabi sauce.

Frederic Couton, Executive Chef
The Cannery Seafood House

Mill Mortadella, Capicolla, Prosciutto and Swiss Panini

Serves: 4

10 inch	Round foccacia bread	25 cm
2 oz.	Mayonnaise	50 g
2 oz.	Pommery mustard	50 g
8 oz.	Swiss cheese	250 g
8 oz.	Mortadella, sliced	250 g
4 oz.	Capicolla, sliced	125 g
4 oz.	Prosciutto	125 g
4 oz.	Leaf lettuce	125 g
4 oz.	Red pepper, roasted	125 g

Slice entire foccacia horizontally in half. Spread bottom half with mayonnaise and mustard. Layer with cheese and meat cuts. Cover with lettuce and red pepper. Replace lid on sandwich and cut into quarters. With oven on broil, or BBQ on a medium setting, toast lightly.

Alexandra Lonsdale, Head Chef
The Mill Marine Bistro

Beet Cured Gravadlax

Serves: 10

26 oz.	Wild salmon fillet, skin on, bones and scales removed	750 g
2 tbsp.	Sea salt, fine grain	30 g
2 tbsp.	White sugar	30 g
1/2 tsp.	White peppercorns, crushed	3 g
1 oz.	Fresh dill tops	25 g
1	Red beet, raw, medium size, peeled and finely grated	1
1 1/2 tbsp.	Pernod (optional)	25 ml

Remove tail end of salmon filet, so that it takes on a more rectangular shape. Lay the salmon filet skin side down in a high-sided dish such as a casserole (note: this dish must be able to have another smaller dish fit within its confines to act as a weighting platform for the salmon).

Combine the sea salt, sugar and crushed white peppercorns and spread evenly atop the salmon flesh. Coarsely chop the dill and spread evenly over the salt mixture. Spread the grated beet on top of the dill. Drizzle with pernod if desired. Place a layer of plastic wrap over the salmon filet, place the smaller dish on top of this, and weigh down with 3-4 tins of canned soup or vegetables (you can also use a brick or any heavy object to provide weight). Place in a refrigerator for 48 hours. Remove and drain of any accumulated liquid every 12 hours.

After 48 hours remove from refrigerator, and scrape off all of the coating mixture. Pat the filet dry and slice on a slight angle, as thinly as possible and serve with rye bread and your favourite dressing.

Dino Gazzola, Executive Chef
Bridges Restaurant

Scallops
with Black Olive Salt, Arugula and Pine Nuts

Serves: 4

7 oz.	Sun-dried black olives (pitted)	200 g
12	Scallops	12
2 tbsp.	Olive oil, for frying	30 ml
1/4 lb.	Arugula or mixed greens	120 g
1	Shallot, finely chopped	1
6 tbsp.	Olive oil, for vinaigrette	90 ml
3 tbsp.	Balsamic vinegar	45 ml
2 tbsp.	Pine nuts, toasted	30 ml
2 oz.	Reggiano cheese	50 g

Prepare one day before. Cook sun-dried black olives in slow oven for one day until dry and crunchy. Blend in a food processor into a coarse powder. Sear the scallops in a hot pan with 2 tbsp. (30 ml) olive oil for 2-3 minutes, to medium rare. Dredge one side in olive powder. Set on arugula, season with balsamic vinaigrette, toasted pine nuts and shaved Reggiano.

Stéphan Meyer, Chef
Piccolo Mondo

Ravioli alle Melanzane
(Eggplant Ravioli)

Serves: 4

Filling

1	Eggplant	1
1 clove	Garlic, chopped	1 clove
1 tsp.	Thyme	5 ml
3 tbsp.	Olive oil	45 ml
to taste	Salt and pepper	to taste
2 tbsp.	Chervil, chopped	30 ml

Split an eggplant lengthwise, score the flesh and season with garlic, thyme, 1 tbsp. (15 ml) olive oil, salt and pepper. Bake at 350°F (180°C) for 45 minutes until soft. Remove the cooked flesh from the skin and chop. Add remaining olive oil, chervil, salt and pepper.

10 oz.	Pasta dough	300 g

Roll out pasta dough (8 oz./220g flour, 2 eggs) as thin as possible into two sheets. On the bottom sheet place 1 tbsp. (15 ml) of filling at 2 inch (5 cm) intervals, making 32 pieces. Cover with second sheet and cut into squares, sealing the edges. Cook in boiling water.

Sauce

7 oz.	Chicken stock	200 ml
5 tbsp.	Tomato, peeled, diced and de-seeded	75 ml
1/2 tbsp.	Butter	7 ml
to taste	Salt and pepper	to taste
3 tbsp.	Olive oil	45 ml
to taste	Chervil leaves	to taste

Bring chicken stock to a boil in a pan, add tomato, butter, salt, pepper, olive oil and cook for 1 minute. Add ravioli and chervil leaves. Heat through and serve.

Stéphan Meyer, Chef
Piccolo Mondo

Goat Cheese and
Roasted Garlic Parcels
with Black Olive Dressing

Serves: 4

4 cloves	Garlic	4 cloves
2	Shallots	2
16 oz.	Goat cheese	450 g
1	Lemon, juiced	1
2 tbsp.	Basil, finely chopped	30 ml
2 tbsp.	Tarragon, finely chopped	30 ml
2 tbsp.	Chives, finely chopped	30 ml
to taste	Salt and pepper	to taste
12	Spring roll wrappers	12
1	Egg, beaten	1
4 cups	Seasonal mixed greens	1 litre

Blanch garlic and shallots in boiling water. Transfer to a heavy roasting pan and roast in a 375°F (190°C) oven until golden brown. Remove from roasting pan, allow to cool and chop finely. In the bowl of an electric mixer put goat cheese, juice of lemon, herbs, garlic, shallot, salt and pepper. Mix at medium speed until blended and creamy. Remove to piping bag. Place one spring roll wrapper on a work surface so that it is in diamond formation. Pipe approximately 1 1/2 tsp. (7 ml) of goat cheese down the centre in a single line. Brush edges with beaten egg and fold the right side to the left and egg wash the remaining sides. Fold the bottom point to the top forming a small triangle. Fry until golden brown in a deep fryer set at 360°F (185°C). Arrange mixed greens on plate and top with 3 parcels per person; drizzle with Black Olive Dressing.

Black Olive Dressing

2 cups	Black olives, pitted	500 ml
2	Anchovy filets	2
1 clove	Garlic	1 clove
7 oz.	Olive oil, good quality	200 ml

Pulse all ingredients in a food processor and refrigerate.

Frank Dodd, Executive Chef
Bacchus Restaurant, Wedgewood Hotel

Mediterranean Quesadilla

Serves: 4

4	Tortillas	4
1 lb.	Grilled chicken, sliced	450 g
4 oz.	Pesto sauce	125 g
8 oz.	Feta cheese	250 g
8 oz.	Red pepper, roasted	250 g
8 oz.	Spinach, sautéed	250 g
8 oz.	Black olives, sliced	250 g

Preheat oven to 350°F (180°C).

On one half of a tortilla evenly spread 1/4 of chicken, pesto sauce, feta, red pepper, spinach and olives. Fold in half and repeat with remaining tortillas. Bake for approximately 7 minutes until crisp. Cut into wedges and serve.

Serving suggestion: Serve with a side of salsa and sour cream.

Alexandra Lonsdale, Head Chef
The Mill Marine Bistro

Spiced Tuna Sushi Spring Roll
with Ginger and Sesame Salad

Serves: 4

1 cup	Sushi rice	250 ml
1 cup	Water	250 ml
to taste	Salt and pepper	to taste
1 tsp.	Sugar	5 ml
4 tsp.	Rice wine vinegar	20 ml
2 sheets	Nori paper	2 sheets
1 tsp.	Wasabi paste	5 ml
1 oz.	Tuna, thinly sliced	30 g
1/4	Yellow pepper, cut into thin strips	1/4
1/4	Red pepper, cut into thin strips	1/4
4	Green onions, sliced	4
	Flour and water to make a paste	
1 package	Spring roll wrappers	1 package

Rinse sushi rice in a chinois (conical strainer) under cold water for about 1/2 hour, then place into a rice cooker with 1 cup of water, salt and pepper for about 15-20 minutes. If you don't have a rice cooker, follow instructions on rice package. Once rice is cooked, spread onto a tray lined with wax paper and drizzle with the sugar and rice wine vinegar mix. Let the rice cool to room temperature.

Cover a bamboo mat with plastic wrap, moisten your hands and evenly pack half of the rice over the mat. Then place the nori sheet over the rice. Along the top edge of the nori sheet, rub a line of wasabi paste and then place a strip of tuna on top of the wasabi line, along with the red and yellow pepper strips and green onion. Then fold the plastic wrap from the top down, just so the rice is touching the nori and pull the wrap back. Take the mat with the plastic wrap and gently roll towards yourself. Once it's rolled up, pick up the whole log and make sure it is round. When you remove the bamboo mat, the sushi will still be wrapped in the plastic wrap. Repeat procedure for second roll. When ready to proceed, remove wrap and cut roll in half.

Mix flour and water together in a small bowl to make a paste. Place

2 sheets of spring roll wrappers beside each other on an angle and along the top edges, spread some flour paste. Centre a half sushi roll at the bottom of each wrapper and fold up bottom corner over the roll, about half way, then fold in the left and right corner towards the centre to make it airtight. Finish rolling upwards and the pasted edge will seal. Repeat this procedure with second sushi roll and more wrappers.

Ginger and Sesame Salad

	Rice noodles	
1/2 cup	Sesame oil	125 ml
to taste	Ginger, finely diced	to taste
to taste	Garlic	to taste
1 1/4 cup	Soya sauce	300 ml
1/4 cup	Rice wine vinegar	50 ml
4 portions	Salad greens	4 portions
1 tbsp.	Sesame seeds	15 ml
to taste	Daikon, julienned	to taste
to taste	Cucumber, seedless, julienned	to taste
	Prawn oil	
	Soya sauce	
	Sesame oil	
	Fresh chives, chopped	

Sauté the ginger and garlic in sesame oil and let cool, then add the soya sauce. When cool, add half of the rice wine vinegar and whisk in the olive oil. Season only with pepper, as the soya sauce is salty.

Pull a small portion of rice noodles apart and place into a deep fryer or hot pan of oil until crisp. Place on some paper towel and season.

Assembly: When ready to serve, first place sushi into hot oil and fry until crispy and golden brown and drain on a paper towel. Then cut at an angle into 6 evenly cut slices and remove both ends. Mix the salad greens with sesame seeds, soya dressing, daikon, and cucumber and place at top of serving plate and top with fried glass noodles. Then place sushi slices around the bottom and garnish with dots of prawn oil, soya sauce, sesame oil and chives.

Robert Byford, Executive Chef
The Beach House

Saskatoon and Blackberry Sauce for Game Meat

Yields: 3 1/2 cups (800 ml)

1 tbsp.	Canola oil	15 ml
2 cloves	Garlic, minced	2 cloves
to taste	Rosemary	to taste
1/2 tsp.	Salt	2 ml
1/2 tsp.	Black pepper, freshly ground	2 ml
2 cups	Saskatoon berries, fresh or frozen **or** 1 1/2 cups (375 ml) Saskatoon berry jam and 1/2 cup (125 ml) water	500 ml
1 cup	Blackberry syrup **or** 1/2 cup (125 ml) strained blackberry purée and 1/2 cup (125 ml) sugar	250 ml
1 cup	Water	250 ml

In a medium sized sauce pan heat oil to medium heat and add garlic, rosemary, salt and pepper. Sauté for 1-2 minutes, do not brown. Add Saskatoon berries and stir for 2 minutes, then add the blackberries, 1 cup (250 ml) of water and bring to a boil. Lower heat and simmer for 15 minutes. Adjust seasoning and sweetness to taste.

2-3 tbsp.	Tapioca starch	30–45 ml
1/2 cup	Water	125 ml

Blend tapioca starch and water, add to berry mix and bring to a rolling boil. Stir for 2 minutes and remove from heat and let cool.

Serving suggestions: This sauce complements caribou and other game meat cuts.

Dolly Watts, Chef/Owner
Liliget Feast House

The Teahouse Stuffed Mushrooms

Serves: 4

Preheat the oven to 350°F (180°C).

24	Mushroom caps, the size of a loonie	24
2 oz.	Butter, melted	55 g
8 oz.	Cream cheese, firm	250 g
1-2	Green onion, chopped	1-2
1 tbsp.	Garlic, minced	15 ml
2 oz.	Emmental cheese, grated	55 g
2 oz.	Dungeness crabmeat	55 g
2 oz.	Shrimp meat	55 g
to taste	Salt and pepper	to taste

Remove the stems from the mushrooms. Place on a cookie sheet and brush the insides with melted butter. Place in the oven at 350°F (180°C) for 10 minutes, take out to cool. Using a mixer, add the cream cheese, garlic, half of the grated emmental, and salt and pepper. Mix until soft. Add crabmeat, shrimp and green onions. Mix by hand. With a teaspoon fill the caps evenly and top with the remaining cheese. Bake for 5 minutes and then broil to melt the cheese. Serve immediately.

Wine suggestion: A perfect wine choice would be a Riesling for the sweeter side, or a Chardonnay for the seafood side.

Lynda Larouche
The Teahouse Restaurant in Stanley Park at Ferguson Point

Walnut-Crusted Goat Cheese
with Red Pepper Coulis

Serves: 4

Red Pepper Coulis

1	Red pepper, seeded and sliced	1
1/2 cup	Red wine vinegar	125 ml
1/4 cup	Sugar	60 ml
1	Shallot, sliced	1

Place red wine vinegar and sugar in a small saucepan with a tight-fitting lid. Bring to a boil on medium-high heat, then add red pepper and shallot. Turn down to low, cover, and simmer until vegetables soften; about 30 minutes. Cool for 15 minutes. Purée in a blender or food processor. Strain and refrigerate.

Walnut-Crusted Goat Cheese

8 oz.	Soft goat cheese	250 g
1/2 cup	Dry bread crumbs	125 ml
1/2 cup	Walnuts	125 ml
	Flour for breading	
1	Egg, beaten lightly	1
1/4 cup	Olive oil	60 ml
	Arugula or baby spring salad greens for garnish	

Divide goat cheese into 4 portions. Form each piece into a small round about 3 inches (7.5 cm) in diameter. Chill thoroughly in the refrigerator. Place bread crumbs and walnuts in a blender or food processor and finely chop. Roll each cheese piece in flour, then dip in beaten egg, and cover with breadcrumb mixture. Heat olive oil in a frying pan on medium heat. Fry breaded cheese pieces until golden all over and heated through; 2 to 3 minutes. Drain on paper towels. Pour 2 tbsp. (30 ml) red pepper coulis to form a small pool on each plate, then place a piece of breaded cheese in the centre. Garnish with a few sprigs of arugula or baby spring salad greens.

Dennis Green, Executive Chef
Bishop's

Ebi Shinjo
(Shrimp Cakes)

Serves: 4

2 tbsp.	Dashi (Bonito stock) **or** chicken **or** fish stock	30 ml
2 tsp.	Carrot, finely diced	10 ml
1/4 cup	Cooking onion, finely chopped	50 ml
2	Fresh shitake mushrooms, large	2
6 oz.	Raw shrimp, large, peeled, deveined and coarsely chopped	170 g
4 oz.	White fish fillet, de-boned, chopped halibut, snapper, **or** cod	125 g
1/2 tsp.	Sea salt	2 ml
1 tsp.	Light shoyu **or** soya sauce	5 ml
2 tsp.	Sugar	10 ml
1	Egg, well beaten	1
2-3 cups	Oil for deep frying	500-750 ml

Put dashi, carrot, onion and mushrooms in a saucepan and sauté over medium heat, until all the vegetables have softened. Set aside to cool. In a mixing bowl combine the chopped shrimp and white fish. Add the cooled vegetable mixture, salt, soya sauce and sugar. With your hand, mix the ingredients together. Add half of the beaten egg and continue to mix well, kneading the mixture to form a sticky paste. Cover with plastic and allow it to rest, refrigerated for 1/2-1 hour. Heat enough oil to deep fry, about 2 inches (5 cm) deep, in a heavy saucepan over low heat to 250°F (130°C). Divide into 4 portions and form into round flat patties, about 1/2-3/4 inch (12-20 mm) thick. Set patties onto a baking sheet lined with wax paper and loosely cover until ready to deep fry. Carefully place the patties into the hot oil and cook for 4-5 minutes. Remove and drain on a baking sheet lined with paper towel. Increase the temperature of the oil to 350°F (180°C) and when ready, add the shrimp patties to the hot oil again and fry 1-2 minutes or until golden brown.

Serving suggestions: May be served with baby mesclun salad greens and a dash of wasabi on the side.

Hidekazu Tojo, Executive Chef/Owner
Tojo's

Tofu Goreng
(Deep Fried Tofu with Spicy Sauce)

Serves: 4

Spicy Sauce

1 tbsp.	Chili garlic sauce	15 ml
1 tbsp.	Hoi san sauce	15 ml
	(Chinese seafood sauce)	
2 tbsp.	White vinegar	30 ml
2 tbsp.	Sugar	30 ml
1 tbsp.	Lime juice	15 ml
2 tbsp.	Roasted peanuts, crushed	30 ml

Prepare the sauce first, mixing all the spicy sauce ingredients together.

Tofu

2 cakes	Tofu	2 cakes
	Oil for deep-frying	
4 oz.	Bean sprouts	125 g
1	Small cucumber, finely shredded	1

Tofu is often cut into triangles but you can choose whatever shape you want. Heat oil and deep fry tofu on both sides until golden brown. Mix together bean sprouts and cucumber.

To serve: Slice tofu pieces in half and stuff with the bean sprouts and cucumber mixture. Drizzle the spicy sauce over the top and serve.

Calvin Chong, Chef/Owner
Banana Leaf Malaysian Restaurant

Mussels Steamed in a Chipotle Cream

Serves: 6

3 lbs.	Mussels, rinsed and de-bearded	1.3 kg
6 tbsp.	Butter	90 ml
1/2	Onion, medium, chopped	1/2
2 tbsp.	Basil, chopped	30 ml
1/4 cup	White wine	50 ml
3 tbsp.	Pernod	45 ml
7 oz.	Chipotle in adobo	200 g
2 cups	Whipping cream	500 ml
1/2 cup	Coconut milk	1/2 cup
	Basil and tomatoes, for garnish	

Sweat onion and basil in butter until onions are translucent. Add white wine, Pernod and chipotles and reduce by half. Add cream and coconut milk and simmer for 10 minutes. Purée the sauce, then strain through a fine mesh strainer. Return the sauce to the heat and bring to a boil. Add mussels and cook uncovered*, stirring often until mussels are cooked; transfer mussels to serving dish. (If the sauce is too thin, continue cooking to reduce.) Adjust seasoning and pour sauce over mussels; garnish with chopped basil and tomatoes.

* The mussels will release their natural nectar when they cook which thins the sauce. If you are cooking 1 lb. (450 g) of mussels or less, they can be covered.

Jonathan Thauberger, Executive Chef
Delilah's

Aaloo Gobi
(Curried Cauliflower and Potato)

Serves: 4

2	Potatoes, medium	2
1	Cauliflower, large	1
2	Onions, medium	2
1	Tomato, medium	1
3	Green chilies, or to taste	3
4 cloves	Garlic	4 cloves
1 inch	Fresh ginger	2.5 cm
1 tbsp.	Vegetable oil	15 ml
1 tbsp.	Canned tomatoes, crushed	15 ml
1/2 tsp.	Ground turmeric	2 ml
1 tsp.	Dhania-jeera Masala* or mild curry paste	5 ml
1 tsp.	Sabzi Masala*	5 ml
1 tsp.	Salt	5 ml
1/2 cup	Green onions, chopped	125 ml

* For spice mixtures, see next page.

To prepare vegetables, peel potatoes and boil until tender. Cut into 1 inch (2.5 cm) dice. Cut cauliflower into bite-sized pieces; steam until tender-crisp and set aside. Coarsely chop onions, dice tomato, slice chilies, finely chop garlic and ginger. Set aside. Heat oil in a large pan over medium heat. Add chopped onion and sauté until tender. Add ginger and garlic and sauté for 1 minute. Add crushed tomatoes, ground turmeric, dhania-jeera, sabzi masala, chilies, raw tomato and salt. Cook for 2 minutes and add vegetables. Mix to coat with spices and continue cooking until vegetables are heated through. The final heating can also be done in the microwave in a covered dish. Garnish with green onions and serve with whole wheat bread or, for a more authentic combination, serve with chapatis.

Krishna Jamal, Executive Chef
Rubina Tandoori

Spice Mixtures

Toasting spices releases their flavours and adds an extra taste element. Use a heavy skillet, preferably without a non-stick surface. Heat the pan over low heat, add all the spices, toss and stir for about 2-4 minutes, as they cook. The minute you smell the toasty fragrance, remove them from the pan. They can be stored in a jar in the freezer.

Classic Indian Masala

Yields: 2/3 cup

6 tbsp.	Coriander seeds	90 ml
3 tbsp.	Cumin seeds	45 ml
1/2 tsp.	Carom seeds	2 ml
1/4	Star anise (2-3 sections)	1/4
3 inch	Cinnamon stick	8 cm
4	Cloves	4
3	Cardamom pods, preferably black	3
4-5	Bay leaves	4-5
1 1/2 tsp.	Dried cilantro	7 ml
1/2 tsp.	Mace	2 ml
1 1/2 tsp.	Ground turmeric	7 ml
1 1/2 tsp.	Powdered red chilies	7 ml

Dhania-jeera Masala

Yields: 2/3 cup

7 tbsp.	Coriander seeds	100 ml
4 tbsp.	Cumin seeds	60 ml

Sabzi Masala

Yields: 2/3 cup

All the ingredients from Classic Masala plus:

2 tsp.	Dhania-jeera	10 ml

Krishna Jamal, Executive Chef
Rubina Tandoori

Classic Steak Side Dishes

Creamed Spinach with Béchamel Sauce
Serves: 6

1/4 lb.	Butter	125 g
1	Small onion, diced	1
1	Bay leaf	1
1 tsp.	Nutmeg	5 ml
3/4 cup	Flour	175 ml
2 cups	Whipping cream	500 ml
3 cups	Milk	750 ml
6	Anchovy fillets, puréed	6
1 bag or package	Spinach, fresh or frozen	1 bag or package
to taste	Salt and white pepper	to taste

To make béchamel sauce, sauté onions and bay leaf in butter. Add nutmeg and flour and cook for 8 minutes. Add whipping cream and milk. Then add puréed anchovies. Bring to a boil stirring constantly. Cool in ice bath if not used immediately.

Cook and drain spinach or squeeze thawed spinach until all excess moisture is removed. Mix in béchamel sauce until thoroughly mixed. Heat mixture in sauté pan, season to taste, then serve.

Dijon Mustard Vinaigrette

Yields: 6 3/4 cups, enough for 2 salad recipes.

1 cup	Dijon mustard	250 ml
1/2 cup	Honey	125 ml
1 1/4 cup	White wine vinegar	300 ml
4 cups	Canola oil	1 litre
to taste	Salt and pepper	to taste

Combine mustard, honey, and vinegar in mixing bowl and whisk while slowly drizzling in the oil. Season with salt and pepper.

Bala Kumanan, Executive Chef
Gotham Steakhouse and Cocktail Bar

Classic Steak Side Dishes
(continued)

Tomato, Onion and Blue Cheese Salad

Serves: 6

5	Tomatoes, large beef steak	5
1	Red onion, medium	1
2 cups	Crumbled Stilton blue cheese	500 ml
3 cups	Dijon Mustard Vinaigrette, see previous page	750 ml

Slice tomatoes 1/2 inch (12 mm) thick. Arrange on platter. Thinly slice red onion and place on top of tomatoes. Then top with cheese and drizzle dressing on top. Season to taste.

Lyonnaise Potatoes

Serves: 6

12	Russet potatoes	12
3	White onions, large	3
1/2 lb.	Duck fat or unsalted butter	225 g
to taste	Salt and white pepper	to taste
1 cup	Parsley, chopped	250 ml

Place unpeeled potatoes in a pot and just cover with water. Boil until just cooked. Remove from water and let cool on tray. Slice onions thinly and sauté over medium heat with 3 oz. (75 g) butter or duck fat until golden brown and caramelized. Peel cooled, cooked potatoes and slice into 1/4 inch (6 mm) slices. Brown sliced potatoes in remaining butter or duck fat until golden, over medium-low heat. Combine browned potatoes and caramelised onions in a sauté pan and heat. Season with salt and white pepper and finish with chopped parsley. When mixture is well incorporated and hot it's done.

Bala Kumanan, Executive Chef
Gotham Steakhouse and Cocktail Bar

Classic Steak Side Dishes
(continued)

Peppercorn Sauce

Yields: approximately 3 cups, enough to serve over six, 9-10 oz. (250-300 g) tenderloin steaks.

2 cups	White wine	500 ml
1 cup	Black peppercorns	250 g
8	Shallots, sliced	8
2	Bay leaves	2
4 cups	Brown stock	1 litre
2 cups	Whipping cream	500 ml
4 oz.	Brandy	125 ml
1/3 cup	Waxy maze*	75 ml
to taste	Salt and white pepper	to taste

Combine white wine, peppercorns, shallots and bay leaves in a sauce pan. Reduce until only a third of the liquid remains, then strain. Add brown stock and reduce by half over medium-low heat. Add cream and reduce by a third. Combine brandy and waxy maze and pour into sauce. Bring to a boil, then simmer for 15 minutes. Season to taste.

* Waxy maze is a commercial thickening agent. Corn starch may be used instead. Adjust amount to thicken appropriately (2-4 tbsp. or 30-60 ml).

Bala Kumanan, Executive Chef
Gotham Steakhouse and Cocktail Bar

Chicken Pakoras

Serves: 12-16

2 lb.	Chicken	900 g

Clean chicken and cut into 12-16 pieces.

Marinade

2 oz.	Plain yogurt	60 g
1/2 oz.	Fresh ginger	15 g
1 tsp.	Salt	5 ml
1 tsp.	Coriander seeds	5 ml
1 tsp.	Dry fenugreek leaves	5 ml
1/2 tsp.	Garam masala	3 ml
2 tsp.	Vinegar	10 ml
12 cloves	Garlic	12 cloves

Combine ingredients. Marinate chicken pieces for 2 hours.

Batter

1	Egg, lightly beaten	1
10 oz.	Flour, gram or split pea	300 g
10 oz.	Flour, all purpose	300 g
1 tbsp.	Water	15 ml
2 tsp.	Lime juice	10 ml
1/2 tsp.	Salt	2 ml
3/4 tsp.	Red pepper flakes	3 ml
1/2 tsp.	Ground coriander	2 ml
1/2 tsp.	Garam masala	2 ml
1 tsp.	Black cumin seeds	5 ml
	Oil for deep-frying	

Beat egg, flours and water together for a few minutes. Add lime juice, salt, red pepper, coriander, garam masala, and cumin. Drain marinade, discard and add chicken to the batter. Stir to make sure all pieces are covered. Set aside for 1/2 hour. Heat oil and deep fry until lightly coloured. Remove chicken pieces and drain on paper towel. Serve with Mint Chutney. (page 30)

Kan Singh, Chef/Owner
Akbar's Own Dining Lounge

Mint Chutney

Yields: 1/2 cup

1 oz.	Tamarind	30 g
4 tbsp.	Water	60 ml
1 oz.	Fresh mint leaves, washed	30 g
1 oz.	Fresh coriander leaves, washed	30 g
1	Green chili	1
1 tsp.	Salt	5 ml
1 1/2 tsp.	White sugar	7 ml

Wash and soak the tamarind for 1/2 hour in 4 tbsp. (60 ml) of water. Put all ingredients in a blender and blend to a fine paste.

Kan Singh, Chef/Owner
Akbar's Own Dining Lounge

Soups
& Salads

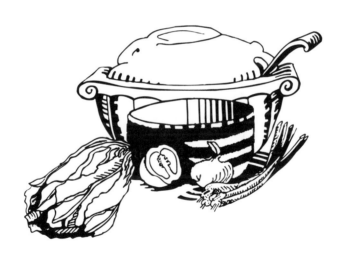

Scallop, Lemongrass and Ginger Soup

Serves: 4

1	Onion, chopped	1
1 stalk	Lemongrass, chopped	1 stalk
4 cloves	Garlic, chopped	4 cloves
small knob	Ginger	small knob
1	Small potato, cubed	1
2 cups	Water	500 ml
3 cups	Cream	750 ml
7 oz.	Scallops	200 g
to taste	Seasoning	to taste

Sweat onions, lemongrass, garlic and ginger without colouring. Add potato, cover with water, bring to a boil and simmer until cooked. Add the cream, bring to a boil and season. Add scallops and remove from heat. Leave standing for 10 minutes, then blend in a food processor and strain through a fine cheese cloth. Keep warm.

Cumin Glaze

1/3 cup	Whipping cream	70 ml
1	Egg yolk, slightly beaten	1
1 tsp.	Cumin, ground	5 ml
to taste	Seasoning, your choice	to taste

Whip cream until it reaches a ribbon consistency and fold in egg yolk and cumin with seasonings.

8	Wonton wrappers, julienned	8
2 oz.	Scallops, diced	50 g
8	Chives, chopped	8

Quickly fry the finely sliced wonton wrappers in a hot frying pan or deep fryer until golden brown and crispy. Drain on paper towel. Place the scallops and chives into bowls. Pour the hot soup over the scallops and chives. Drizzle with cumin glaze and caramelize under a broiler or with a blow torch. Sprinkle with the crispy fried wontons.

Robert Byford, Executive Chef
The Beach House

Red Cabbage Slaw

Serves: 12-15

4 cups	White vinegar	1 litre
1/2 cup	Sugar	125 ml
1 cup	Raspberry syrup	250 ml
1 tsp.	Salt	5 ml
1 tsp.	Pepper	5 ml
1/2 tsp.	Cinnamon, ground	2 ml
1/2 tsp.	Allspice	2 ml
1/2 cup	Red wine or blackberry syrup	125 ml
3 small	Red cabbage heads, shredded	3 small
1 1/2 cups	Craisins (dried cranberries)	375 ml

Combine all ingredients except red cabbage and craisins in a pan and bring to a boil. Pour dressing over cabbage and mix well with craisins.

Dolly Watts, Chef/Owner
Liliget Feast House

Fraser Valley Quail Salad
with Goat Cheese and Caramel Poached Pears

Serves: 6

4 oz.	Mixed mushrooms, fresh	120 g
2 tsp.	Mixed herbs	10 ml
	Olive oil, for cooking and dressing	

Sauté the mushrooms in olive oil, season and then add the fresh herbs. Place them in a warm spot of the kitchen until they are needed.

6	Boneless quails (supreme and boneless legs)	6
1/4 cup	Chicken stock	50 ml
1 tbsp.	Aged balsamic vinegar	15 ml
2 tbsp.	Sherry vinegar	30 ml
6 pieces	Goat cheese, small pieces (preferably local and a creamy type)	6 pieces
6	Small croutons	6

Sear the quail legs (both sides) and then the breast (skin side only) in a non-reactive frying pan. Place them in a very hot oven 400°F (200°C) for a couple of minutes and then remove from the pan; deglaze with the chicken stock. Add the vinegars and a touch of olive oil (this will be the dressing). Place the goat cheese on the croutons and warm up in the oven very quickly.

Caramel Poached Pears

3	Pears (preferably a small variety)	3
1 1/2 oz.	Sugar	40 g
2 tsp.	Butter	10 ml

Preheat oven to 350°F (180°C). To poach the pears, make a caramel by pouring the sugar into a heavy-bottomed pot over medium-low heat. Allow the sugar to melt, without stirring, until it is at the blonde stage. Add the cored and peeled pears. At this point the caramel will stop cooking and the pears will release their juices. Cover and bake in the oven for 8–10 minutes. Remove the pears from the caramel and stir the butter into the sauce. Return the pears to the caramel and let cool.

Assembly: Place the mushrooms in the centre of the plate. Place the goat cheese to one side and the pear half with the caramel sauce opposite. Place the quail breast and legs with the dressing in the middle to finish the dish.

Wine suggestions: I find that a rich white such as Striped Label Blue Mountain Chardonnay or a light red such as Striped Label Blue Mountain Pinot Noir work exceptionally well with this dish.

Pino Posteraro, Executive Chef/Owner
Cioppino's

Larb Gai

Serves: 2-3

Larb is an easy to make spicy dish served throughout Thailand. Use beef (larb nuea) or pork (larb moo) as alternatives to chicken.

4 oz.	Chicken breast, minced	150 g
2-3 tbsp.	Chicken stock	30-45 ml
2-3 tbsp.	Lemon juice	30-45 ml
2 tbsp.	Fish sauce	30 ml
1 tbsp.	Sugar	15 ml
1 tsp.	Dried chilies, ground	5 ml
1 tbsp.	Khao koor *	15 ml
10 leaves	Fresh mint, shredded	10 leaves
3-4	Shallots or red onions, chopped (1/2 cup or 125 ml)	3-4
3	Kaffir lime leaves, shredded	3
2	Green onion stalks	2
5 leaves	Cilantro, shredded	5 leaves
garnish	Fancy lettuce and mint leaves,	garnish

Line a serving dish with lettuce leaves. Heat the chicken stock at high heat in a wok. Stir fry the chicken until it just starts to turn whitish. Add all the remaining ingredients and stir until the chicken is cooked.

*Khao koor: heat a medium-sized wok to fairly hot and add a few tablespoons of uncooked rice. Stir until golden brown. Remove from heat and cool. With a spice mill, mortar and pestle or a blender, grind to a fairly coarse powder, retaining some texture.

Serving suggestion: Serve on a bed of lettuce leaves and garnish to taste. Serve with sticky rice or use Thai jasmine rice and a dish of mixed raw vegetables. To eat, take a small ball of sticky rice in the fingers and use it to pick up a little larb, and then eat it with the raw veggies. You can also use a fork and spoon as a lot of Thais do.

Siriwan (Grace) Rerksuttisiridach, Executive Chef/Owner
Simply Thai Restaurant

Minestrone Soup
with Spicy Cheese Straws

Serves: 4

2 tbsp.	Olive oil	30 ml
4 cloves	Garlic, finely chopped	4 cloves
1	Red onion, chopped	1
1 tbsp.	Fresh thyme	15 ml
2	Carrots, chopped	2
6 stalks	Celery, chopped	6 stalks
1	Small turnip, small cubes	1
1 cup	Cabbage, chopped	250 ml
18 oz.	Stewed tomatoes, canned	500 ml
8 cups	Chicken stock	2 litres
1/2 cup each	Chick peas and kidney beans	125 ml each
1 cup	Small shaped pasta, precooked	250 ml
to taste	Salt and pepper	to taste

In a heavy bottomed pot, add olive oil and sauté garlic, onion, and herbs until transparent but not browned. Add remaining vegetables and sauté, stirring constantly. Add tomatoes and chicken stock, bring to a low boil and simmer for 20 minutes. Add remaining ingredients and simmer for another 10 minutes. Adjust seasoning and serve with cheese straws.

Spicy Cheese Straws

1 lb.	Puff pastry	500 g
1/2 tsp. each	Paprika and cayenne pepper	2 ml each
8 tbsp.	Parmesan cheese	120 ml
1	Egg yolk, beaten	1

Roll dough into a thin sheet and sprinkle with half of the paprika, cayenne and cheese. Turn sheet over and sprinkle with remaining spices and cheese. Place in a freezer for 20-30 minutes to harden. Cut into 1/2 inch (12 mm) strips with a pizza wheel. Twist into spirals. Place on an ungreased cookie sheet, pressing ends down so they won't unravel during baking. Bake for 12 minutes at 350°F (180°C)

Frank Dodd, Executive Chef
Bacchus Restaurant, Wedgewood Hotel

Warm Mixed Green Salad

Serves: 2

2 portions	Mixed green salad	2 portions
to taste	Shredded carrot	to taste
1/4 lb.	Mushrooms, sliced	120 g
1/2	English cucumber, sliced	1/2

Dressing

1 cup	Soy sauce	250 ml
1/4 cup	Sesame oil	50 ml
1/8 cup	Ginger, finely chopped	25 ml
dash	Pepper, freshly ground	dash
1/8 cup	Teriyaki sauce	25 ml
2	Green onion, diced	2
1/8 cup	Sesame seeds	25 ml

Mix together and heat up.

Serving suggestion: Arrange salad ingredients on a cold plate and pour the dressing on top. Serve immediately.

Richard Taoukil, Executive Chef
Prospect Point Restaurant

Baby Spinach, Pine Nut and Goat Cheese Salad
Topped with Grilled Asparagus

Serves: 4

Salad

4 portions	Baby spinach	4 portions
2 oz.	Croutons	55 g
2 oz.	Pine nuts, toasted	55 g
	Asparagus, grilled for garnish	

Gently toss all ingredients, except asparagus in a bowl.

Goat Cheese

8 oz.	Goat cheese	300 g
to taste	Rosemary, thyme, basil, marjoram	to taste

In a mixing bowl, soften the cheese and mix with chopped herbs.

Dressing

1/3 cup	Balsamic vinegar	70 ml
6 oz.	Extra virgin oil	175 ml
to taste	Salt and pepper	to taste

Reduce the balsamic vinegar in a small pan by about half and transfer to a mixing bowl and leave to cool slightly. Then whisk in olive oil slowly. As it starts to emulsify, add a little water to thin out so the dressing stays the right consistency, and season.

Assembly: Toss salad with goat cheese and dressing. Place in the centre of serving plate and garnish with grilled asparagus.

Robert Byford, Executive Chef
The Beach House

Chilled Avocado Soup
with Dungeness Crab Meat
and Jalapeño Sorbet

Serves: 8

Jalapeño Sorbet

7 oz.	Sugar	200 g
2 cups	Water	500 ml
5	Lemons, juiced	5
1	Jalapeño pepper	1
2 oz.	Tequila	60 ml

To make the sorbet, you will need an ice cream machine, however if you don't have one, you can substitute with lemon sorbet and add tequila with the cream garnish at the end. (Make sure the sorbet is not too sweet.)

In a sauce pot, mix the sugar, water and lemon juice. Cut the jalapeño pepper in half and remove the seeds from one half, so the sorbet will not be too spicy. Add the other half of jalapeño (with the seeds) to the pot and bring to boil for one minute. Set aside to cool down. Remove the infused jalapeño pepper and add the tequila. Put the sorbet liquid in a blender and add the remaining pepper without the seeds. Mix well and pour the liquid into the ice cream machine. Process until set and freeze the sorbet for one hour. Make 8 scoops and keep them frozen until serving.

Tortillas

8	Blue corn tortillas, 4 inch (10 cm) diameter	8

Put the corn tortillas, one at a time, into a deep fryer at 300°F (150°C) and, with a small ladle, shape each into a cup. Deep-fry for 2 minutes. Remove and place on a paper towel to absorb excess oil. Reserve for the sorbet.

Avocado Soup

6	Avocados, ripe	6
2	Limes, juiced	2
3 cups	Vegetable stock	750 ml
to taste	Salt and pepper	to taste
1 cup	Whipping cream	250 ml
4 oz.	Dungeness crab meat	120 g
2 tbsp.	Cilantro, sliced	30 ml

Peel the avocados, remove and discard the pits. Cut the avocado meat into cubes and put in a blender. Add lime juice, vegetable stock, salt and pepper. Blend until liquefied to a smooth consistency. Add 1/2 of the cream and save the rest for garnish. Season to taste and set aside.

Assembly: Pour the soup into 8 soup bowls. Add the crab meat and sprinkle with the sliced cilantro. Place the jalapeño sorbet in the blue corn tortilla cups and place in the centre of the soup. Finish with a drizzle of cream all around the soup and serve.

Frederic Couton, Executive Chef
The Cannery Seafood House

Creamy Westcoast Clam Chowder
with Smoked Sockeye Salmon

Serves: 12-16

This is The Mill Marine Bistro's signature dish.

1/2 lb.	Onion, chopped	225 g
4 oz.	Celery	125 g
1 oz.	Butter	25 g
2 oz.	Flour	55 g
3 1/4 cups	Fish stock	750 ml
4 1/2 cups	Clams, canned with liquid	1 litre
10 oz.	Potatoes, small dice	300 g
2 cups	Milk	500 ml
1/2 cup	Cream	125 ml
8 oz.	Smoked sockeye salmon	250 g
to taste	Salt and pepper	to taste
to taste	Worcestershire sauce	to taste
to taste	Thyme	to taste

Sauté onions and celery in butter. Add flour and cook to make a blonde roux. Add stock and whisk to remove any lumps. Add clams with liquid to pot. Stir well and add potato, milk, cream and smoked salmon. Simmer on low heat until potatoes are cooked. Season to taste with remaining ingredients.

Alexandra Lonsdale, Head Chef
The Mill Marine Bistro

Fraser Valley Micro Greens
with Seared Grapes and Verjus Vinaigrette

Serves: 6

15	Grapes, seedless, red or green	15
3	Shallots, medium, very finely sliced	3
2 tbsp.	Brown sugar	30 ml
1 cup	Grape verjus*, red or white	250 ml
1/4 cup	Chicken stock	50 ml
3 sprigs	Thyme	3 sprigs
1/2 cup	Oil, olive or grapeseed	1/2 cup
to taste	Salt and pepper, freshly ground	to taste
6 portions	Salad greens	6 portions

Preheat sauté pan to a medium temperature and coat the bottom with a small amount of oil. When the pan is hot but not smoking, add the grapes and sear for no more than a minute. The grapes should shrivel slightly and become golden brown. Remove the grapes and sauté the shallots in the same pan. When the shallots have caramelized slightly and are a consistent golden colour, add the sugar. The brown sugar will begin to melt, giving a deep caramel depth to the dressing. Before the sugar burns add the verjus and reduce, without boiling until there is about 1/4 cup of liquid left in the pan. Add the chicken stock and again reduce, at a simmer, for a few minutes or until the liquid begins to take body and is slightly syrupy. Remove leaves of thyme from the stems and chop finely. Add to the pan. Turn the heat off. Add the oil and then season to desired taste.

Drizzle the dressing, either warm or cold, over your choice of lettuce, add seared grapes, toss and serve.

* Verjus is the unfermented juice of unripe grapes and other unripe fruit. Its flavour has the tartness of lemon and the acidity of vinegar without the harshness of either. Look for verjus at your local specialty food store or Middle Eastern grocery store. An alternative is to mix equal amounts of grape juice with cider vinegar.

Sylvain Cuerrier, Executive Chef
The Observatory Restaurant at Grouse Mountain

THE OBSERVATORY RESTAURANT AT
GROUSE MOUNTAIN

Roasted Butternut Squash Soup
with Chinese Five Spiced Scallops

Serves: 8

1/2 cup	Butter	125 ml
2	White onions, medium, diced	2
8 cloves	Garlic, diced	8 cloves
2	Carrots, diced	2
1	Butternut squash, medium, diced	1
1/2 cup	Brown sugar	125 ml
5-6 sprigs	Fresh thyme leaves	5-6 sprigs
11 cups	Chicken stock	2.5 litres
1 cup	Heavy cream	250 ml
to taste	Salt, white pepper, Tabasco	to taste

Melt the butter in a heavy-bottomed soup pot and sweat the onions and garlic. Without browning the onions, cook for a few minutes. Add the carrots and squash and sautée until they become tender. Add sugar and thyme leaves, and cook until the sugar has melted and the vegetables are shiny. Add stock and bring to a boil. Turn heat down and simmer for about 1/2 hour. Add cream and blend thoroughly. Strain through a fine sieve and adjust seasoning.

Five Spiced Scallops

4	Anise seeds	4
10	Fennel seeds	10
1 1/2 tsp.	Cinnamon	7 ml
1	Clove	1
3	Pepper corns	3
2 tbsp.	Vegetable oil	30 ml
8	Fresh scallops, large	8

Combine all spices in a grinder and blend to a powder. Preheat a sauté pan on medium heat, and coat the bottom with vegetable oil. Toss the scallops with the spice blend. Sear the scallops on both sides for a minute or until they take on a rich golden brown colour. Ladle soup into bowls and garnish each with a seared scallop.

Sylvain Cuerrier, Executive Chef
The Observatory Restaurant at Grouse Mountain

Golden Potato and Sunchoke Soup

Serves: 16

1	Leek, sliced (white and pale green part only)	1
1	Yellow onion, medium, sliced	1
1	Celery rib, sliced	1
1/4 cup	Butter, clarified	50 ml
2 cloves	Garlic, minced	2 cloves
4 lbs.	Yukon Gold potatoes, peeled, diced	1.8 kg
1 lb.	Sunchokes, peeled	450 g
15 cups	Chicken stock	3.5 litres
1/2 cup	Whipping cream, 36%	125 ml
to taste	Salt, white pepper, lemon juice Smoked salmon strips and minced chives for garnish	to taste

In a large pot, slowly sweat the leek, onion and celery in clarified butter. When soft, add the garlic and continue cooking until soft. Add the potatoes, sunchokes and stock. Season lightly with salt and bring to a simmer. Cook until potatoes are soft and then add the cream. Simmer for another 5 minutes, then purée. Pass through a fine chinois and season with salt, white pepper and lemon juice.

Serving suggestion: Serve with fresh bread and a green salad. Garnish with small strips of smoked salmon and minced chives.

James Walt, Executive Chef
Blue Water Café and Raw Bar

Bean Sprout Salad

Serves: 4

Indian bean sprouts are not the same as Chinese bean sprouts, even though they are both made from mung beans. Indian ones barely sprout. Germination takes about a day and a half, and directions are here in the recipe. If you are in a hurry you can substitute the easy-to-find Chinese bean sprouts. They will have a slightly different taste.

1 cup	Mung beans (moong beans)	250 ml
3/4 inch	Fresh ginger	2 cm
1	Cucumber, small	1
1	Slice of cantaloupe, thin	1
1	Green chili or banana pepper	1
1/2 tsp.	Black pepper, coarsely ground	2 ml
1/4 tsp.	Salt	1 ml
2 tsp.	Lemon juice	10 ml

Rinse beans and soak overnight or 12 hours. Drain water, wrap beans in a damp towel and let germinate for 24 hours. Sprinkle water over the towel if it dries out. When the beans have split and about 1/4 inch (5 mm) of sprout is visible, remove from towel. Rinse with cold water and drain. Put in a salad bowl. Grate ginger, dice cucumber and cantaloupe. Thinly slice chili into wheels, removing the seeds. Add chili, pepper, ginger, lemon juice and salt to bean sprouts. Fold in cucumber and cantaloupe and chill for 30 minutes before serving.

Krishna Jamal, Executive Chef
Rubina Tandoori

Cucumber and Winter Melon Salad

Serves: 4

1/2 cup	Vegetable oil	125 ml
1 tsp.	Paprika	5 ml
1 tsp.	Red chilies, cracked	5 ml
2 cloves	Garlic, crushed	2 cloves
1	English cucumber, and an equal amount winter melon, peeled	1
1 tbsp.	Sambal oelek	15 ml
1/3 cup	Mirin*	75 ml
1/3 cup	Rice wine vinegar	75 ml
1	Lime, juiced	1
2 tbsp.	Pickled ginger, finely julienned	30 ml
1 tsp.	Salt	5 ml
1 tsp.	Sugar	5 ml
8 leaves	Sui choy	8 leaves
2 cups	Pea shoots	500 ml
1/2 bunch	Scallions, julienned	1/2 bunch
1/2 cup	Crystallized ginger, julienned	125 ml
1 tbsp.	White sesame seeds	15 ml
1 tbsp.	Black sesame seeds	15 ml

Heat vegetable oil on medium-high heat with the paprika, chilies and the garlic until garlic browns and chilies sizzle. Remove from heat, strain and let cool. Cut cucumber and winter melon into batons the size and width of your pinky finger. Combine the sambal, mirin, rice wine vinegar, lime juice, pickled ginger, salt and sugar in a medium-sized mixing bowl and marinate the cucumber and melon in the mixture for 2 hours or for the best results, overnight. Line 4 salad bowls with 2 sui choy leaves each. Divide cucumber and melon mixture equally into bowls. Heat the strained chili oil in a small pan until it just starts to smoke, and pour over the salads. Garnish with pea shoots, julienned scallions, crystallized ginger, white and black sesame seeds.

* Mirin is a low alcohol, sweet rice wine that is readily available.

Stuart Irving, Chef
Wild Rice

Spring Pea Soup

Serves: 5

3 1/2 oz.	Fresh snap peas	100 g
14 oz.	Frozen peas	400 g
2	Shallots, large	2
1 stalk	Celery	1 stalk
1 clove	Garlic	1 clove
2 2/3 cups	Chicken stock	600 ml
1 sprig	Dill	1 sprig
1 sprig	Parsley	1 sprig
2 tbsp.	Butter	30 ml
to taste	Lemon juice	to taste
to taste	Salt and pepper	to taste

Blanch the snap peas in salted boiling water until slightly crunchy and plunge into ice water. Do the same for the frozen peas. In a large saucepot, sweat the shallots, garlic and celery being careful not to colour the vegetables. Add the chicken stock, dill and parsley and boil for 10 minutes. In a blender combine the stock, peas, butter and snap peas, saving some snap peas for a garnish. Pass through a fine chinois into an ice bath.

To serve: Serve chilled.

Bradley Miller, Chef
Pastis

Endive Salad

Serves: 4

4 heads	Belgian endive	4 heads
1 cup	Baby red chard	250 ml
7 oz.	Walnuts	200 g
2 tsp.	Honey	20 ml
5 tsp.	Hazelnut butter	25 ml
1 tbsp.	Dijon mustard	15 ml
1/4 cup	Sherry vinegar	50 ml
1/2 cup	Hazelnut oil	125 ml
1/4 cup	Canola oil	50 ml
2 tsp.	Water	20 ml
5 oz.	Roquefort, crumbled	150 g
1	Pear, sliced	1
1	Shallot, chopped	1
2 tbsp.	Parsley and chives, chopped	30 ml
to taste	Salt and pepper	to taste

Heat a large pan with a little oil and add the walnuts. Toast them lightly being careful not to burn the nuts. Add honey to taste, season with salt and remove from the heat. Spread the nuts on a baking sheet and leave them to air dry.

In a blender combine the hazelnut butter, mustard and vinegar. Slowly add the oils using the water to adjust the thickness of the emulsification. Season the vinaigrette with salt and pepper.

In a large salad bowl combine the chopped endive, baby chard, Roquefort, pear, candied nuts, shallots and herbs. Toss in vinaigrette and serve.

Bradley Miller, Chef
Pastis

Cream of Celeriac Soup

Serves: 6

1 lb	Celeriac (celery root)	450 g
6 tbsp.	Butter	90 ml
1	Onion, medium, chopped	1
1	Potato, medium, chopped	1
3 ribs	Celery, chopped	3 ribs
1/2 head	Fennel	1/2 head
1/4 cup	Pernod	50 ml
1/4 cup	White wine	50 ml
6 cups	Chicken or vegetable stock	1.4 litres
1/4 tsp.	Fennel seeds	1 ml
1 stalk	Lemongrass, smashed with mallet, not chopped	1 stalk
1/2 cup	Whipping cream (optional)	125 ml
to taste	Lemon juice, salt and pepper	to taste

Peel celeriac and chop coarsely. Squeeze lemon juice over celeriac and cover with cold water. Coarsely chop other vegetables and sauté with butter and 1 tsp. (5 ml) salt until onions are translucent. Add Pernod and wine and reduce by half. Add celeriac and lemon water the celeriac was in and reduce by half. Add chicken stock, fennel seed and lemongrass, bring to a boil and simmer until all vegetables are soft. Remove lemongrass and discard. Purée soup and pass through a fine mesh strainer; return to the pot, bring to a simmer. Adjust the seasoning and add cream. Divide among bowls and garnish the soup with optional ingredients listed below.

Garnish (optional)

1	Granny Smith apple, sliced	1
4 tbsp.	Sugar	60 ml
4 tbsp.	Brandy or Calvados, Sherry, etc.	60 ml
	Truffle oil	

Jonathan Thauberger, Executive Chef
Delilah's

Daily Clipped and Locally Grown Lettuces
with Vanilla, Star Anise and Pineapple Vinaigrette and Buckwheat Slate Stone Fruit Wedges

Serves: 8

Vinaigrette

2	Vanilla beans, split	2
4	Star anise	4
3 cups	Fresh pineapple juice	750 ml
1	Shallot, small, roughly chopped	1
1/2 cup	Grapeseed oil	125 ml
1/4 cup	Champagne vinegar	50 ml
to taste	Salt and white pepper	to taste

Scrape out vanilla bean seeds and place in a saucepan, with star anise, shallot and pineapple juice. Cook over low heat and reduce by half. Whisk in grapeseed oil and vinegar. Season and set aside.

Buckwheat Slate

3/4 cup	Buckwheat flour	175 ml
1/4 cup	Oats	50 ml
1 tbsp.	Plain yogurt	30 ml
1/4 cup	Buttermilk	50 ml
1 cup	Crumbled halva	250 ml
to taste	Salt, and water to bind if needed	to taste

Preheat oven to 350°F (180°C). Combine all ingredients to form dough. Roll on a flat surface to about 1/16 inch (1 mm) thick. Bake on parchment paper and until crispy and golden. Once it has cooled break into pieces the size of a small salad plate.

5 oz. each	Baby lettuce mix	140 g each
1 fruit	Seasonal stone fruit (nectarines,	1 fruit
per serving	plums, etc.) with stones removed	per serving

To serve: Toss lettuce with vinaigrette. Cut fruit into wedges. Place a Buckwheat Slate on a plate, top with dressed lettuce and garnish with stone fruit wedges.

Tina Fineza, Chef
Bin 942 Restaurant

Grilled Asparagus Salad

Serves: 4

Vinaigrette

1 tsp.	Honey	5 ml
2 tbsp.	Balsamic vinegar	30 ml
6 tbsp.	Olive oil, extra virgin	80 ml
2 tsp.	Fresh lemon juice	10 ml
to taste	Salt and white pepper	to taste
2 tbsp.	Shallots, finely chopped	30 ml
2 lb.	Green asparagus	900 g
	Olive oil for grilling	
8 slices	Prosciutto	8 slices
4 oz.	Parmesan, sliced	125 g
1/2 tsp.	Peppercorns, black cracked	2 ml
	Micro greens to garnish	

Heat grill to medium-high. In a stainless steel bowl mix honey and vinegar. Whisking continuously, slowly add olive oil until emulsified. Add lemon juice and season with salt and white pepper. Add shallots and refrigerate until ready to use.

Asparagus

Snap or cut off fibrous ends off asparagus. Bring a large pot of salted water to a boil. Blanch asparagus for one minute and immediately plunge stalks into ice water to stop the cooking process and preserve colour. Place the asparagus on a paper towel to dry. In a stainless steel bowl, toss asparagus with a little olive oil to coat. This will prevent the asparagus from sticking to the grill. Season the asparagus with salt and ground white pepper and place lengthwise on the heated grill. Cooking time will be short, only 1-2 minutes, as asparagus is already pre-cooked. When done, divide asparagus among four plates and spoon vinaigrette over and around asparagus. Place two slices of prosciutto on top. With a vegetable peeler or a sharp knife thinly slice Parmesan into curls and place over prosciutto. Finish with a little coarse black pepper and a few micro greens for garnish. Serve immediately.

Robert Feenie, Executive Chef
Lumière Restaurant

Ceviche Salad

Serves: 3

1 oz.	Vegetable oil	30 g
8 oz.	Snapper fillets	250 g
1	Tomato	1
1	Avocado	1
8 oz.	Baby shrimp, peeled, de-veined, chopped	250 g
3 tbsp.	Corn kernels	45 ml
2 tbsp.	Fresh basil, chopped	30 ml
2 tbsp.	Fresh cilantro, chopped	30 ml
to taste	Salt and pepper	to taste
1/4 cup	Lemon juice	50 ml
1/4 cup	Olive oil	50 ml
3oz.	Mixed green lettuce	85 g
garnish	Lemon juice and lime slices	garnish

Heat vegetable oil in a pan. Dice the fresh snapper in 1/2 inch (1 cm) squares and sauté in the hot oil until slightly cooked. Remove from the pan and season with salt and pepper and let it cool. Meanwhile, dice the tomato and the avocado and set aside. In a glass container mix together snapper, shrimp meat, avocado and tomatoes, corn, and herbs. Toss everything with the lemon juice and olive oil. Season with enough salt and pepper.

Serving suggestion: Place a handful of the lettuce on a plate and top with a generous amount of the seafood mixture. Pour some more lemon juice over everything and garnish with a wedge of lime. Serve cold.

This salad is perfect for a light lunch or an appetizer. It can be served with a slice of fresh bread.

Pablo Rojas, Chef/Owner
Baru Latino Restaurant

Sancocho de Gallina
Traditional Colombian Chicken Soup

Serves: 6-8

3 1/2 lb	Chicken	1.5 kg
1	Onion	1
1	Carrot	1
2	Celery stalks	2
4	Corn on the cob, halved	4
1	Yucca, large, peeled, julienned	1
2	Russet potatoes, peeled, diced	2
1/2 cup	Cilantro leaves	125 ml
2	Avocados	2
1 cup	Shredded mozzarella	250 ml
2	Limes, cut into wedges	2
2 cups	Hogo (recipe below)	500 ml

Cover chicken, onions, carrot, celery in a large pot with 3 quarts (3 litres) of water and salt to taste. Simmer uncovered for 45 minutes, skimming the top. Remove chicken and cool. Strain and reserve broth. Remove meat from chicken, discard bones. Cook corn for 10 minutes in broth. Add yucca, potatoes and half of the cilantro. Season with salt and pepper, simmer until cooked.

Hogo

2 tbsp.	Canola oil	30 ml
1	Yellow onion, large, chopped	1
3	Tomatoes, diced	3
1 bunch	Green onions, chopped	1 bunch
2 tbsp	Tomato paste	30 ml
1 tsp	Garlic, chopped	5 ml

Heat oil and cook onions until transparent. Add tomato and green onions, cook for 5 minutes. Add garlic, tomato paste and mix well. Add salt and pepper and cook 5 minutes. Keep warm.

Assembly: Divide mozzarella, Hogo, avocado evenly and place into individual bowls. Add the broth, making sure each bowl has potatoes, yucca and corn. Top with chicken, cilantro and lime.

Pablo Rojas, Chef/Owner
Baru Latino Restaurant

Entrées

Talay Pad Pong Kari
(Seafood Curry)

Serves: 2-3

This mild curry can be prepared with a mixture of seafood (prawns, squid, mussels, scallops) or crab claws.

5 tbsp.	Oil	75 ml
1 tbsp.	Garlic, chopped into small pieces	15 ml
5	Mussels	5
5	Medium scallops	5
5	Prawns	5
1/4 cup	Squid, sliced	50 ml
1/8 cup	White onion, thinly sliced	30 ml
1/8 cup	Green and red bell pepper, julienned	30 ml
1/4 cup	Chicken stock	50 ml
1 tbsp.	Light soya sauce	15 ml
1 tbsp.	Oyster sauce	15 ml
2 tbsp.	Fish sauce	30 ml
1 tbsp.	Sugar	15 ml
1 cup	Coconut milk (**or** if allergic to coconut milk, use half & half cream)	250 ml
1 tbsp.	Curry powder	15 ml
1	Egg, beaten	1
1/4 cup	Fresh Thai basil	50 ml
1/8 cup	Green onion, thinly sliced	30 ml
	Basil and cucumber slices for garnish	

Heat the oil in a wok and stir-fry the garlic, then add all seafood. Stir-fry until cooked, then add the white onion, green and red bell peppers and mix. Next add the chicken stock, soy sauce, oyster sauce, fish sauce and sugar. Add coconut milk and curry powder; bring to boil, then add the egg. Stir in the Thai basil and green onion.

Serving suggestions: Serve in a serving platter and garnish with basil and slices of cucumber. Eat with steamed Thai jasmine rice.

Siriwan (Grace) Rerksuttisiridach, Executive Chef/Owner
Simply Thai Restaurant

Seared Fillet of Albacore Tuna
with Ragout of Peas and Syrah Sauce

Serves: 6

3 cups	Spring peas	750 ml
3 slices	Double smoked bacon, cut into small strips	3 slices
6 x 6-8 oz.	Albacore tuna medallions, sashimi grade	6 x 175-225g
to taste	Salt and pepper	to taste
6 sprigs	Rosemary	6 sprigs
6	Scallions, sliced	6

Make ragout first: lightly sauté bacon with peas and keep warm. Season the medallions of tuna on both sides and quickly sear them in a non-reactive, non-stick frying pan with rosemary sprigs and the fresh scallions. Cook the tuna gently to rare.

Syrah Sauce

7 oz.	Syrah wine	200 ml
2	Shallots, chopped	2
2	Oranges, one segmented and one juiced	2
	Herb bouquet	
1/4 cup	Fish fumet	50 ml
1 1/2 oz.	Butter	40 g
6 each	Black and green olives, pitted	6 each
6	Cherry tomatoes, peeled	6

Reduce the wine with shallots, orange juice and the herbs. Add the fumet, reduce some more and then remove the bouquet of herbs and whisk in the cold butter. Add the orange segments, pitted olives and the cherry tomatoes. Reserve the sauce in a warm place.

Assembly: Serve with ragout of peas in the center. Place tuna on top; add a rosemary sprig and scallion to each plate. Drizzle with the Syrah Sauce.

Wine suggestion: Burrowing Owl Syrah

Pino Posteraro, Executive Chef/Owner
Cioppino's

Kingfish Marinated in Cabernet Sauvignon with Verdi Risotto

Serves: 4

Kingfish

1 lb.	Kingfish, 1 1/2 inch (4 cm) cubes	450 g
4/5 cup	Cabernet Sauvignon	200 ml
2 sprigs	Thyme	2 sprigs
1/4 tbsp.	Cracked pepper	4 ml
2 cloves	Garlic	2 cloves
1	Shallot	1

Combine all ingredients and marinate for 24 hours. Drain well.

Sauce

3 tbsp.	Butter	45 ml
2	Shallots, minced	2
1 1/4 cups	Cabernet Sauvignon	300 ml
1 cup	Fish stock	250 ml
3 sprigs	Thyme	3 sprigs
2 cups	Beef demi-glaze	500 ml
to taste	Salt and pepper	to taste

Sauté shallots in 1 tbsp. (15 ml) butter. Add red wine and reduce by three quarters. Add fish stock and reduce by three quarters. Add thyme and beef demi-glaze, reduce by a third. Adjust seasoning and whisk in remaining butter.

Verdi Risotto

1 tbsp.	Butter	15 ml
1	Shallot, minced	1
1/2 cup	Whipping cream	100 ml
1 3/4 cups	Arborio rice, precook as you would *al dente* pasta	400 ml
1/4 cup	Herb coulis, following recipe	50 ml
1 oz.	Parmesan cheese	30 g
to taste	Salt and pepper	to taste

Sauté shallots in butter. Add cream and rice. When it begins to thicken add Herb Coulis, Parmesan, salt and pepper. Set aside

Herb Coulis

1/4 bunch	Parsley, leaves only	1/4 bunch
1/2 bunch	Basil, leaves only	1/2 bunch
1 clove	Garlic	1 clove
4 1/2 tbsp.	Olive oil	70 ml

Combine herbs and garlic in blender and slowly add oil.

Assembly: Prepare risotto and sauce, set aside and keep warm. Meanwhile sear marinated Kingfish over medium-high heat until cooked to your preference.

Frederic Couton, Executive Chef
The Cannery Seafood House

Roasted Halibut
with Poached Baby Leeks
and Chanterelle Ragout

Serves: 4

Halibut

4 x 5-6 oz.	Halibut fillets	4 x 140-170 g
to taste	Kosher salt	to taste
to taste	Roasted black pepper	to taste
4 pieces	Unsalted butter	4 pieces
	Butter for coating roasting pan	

Preheat the oven to 400°F (200 °C).

Clean fish by removing all skin, bones and excess fat. Fillets should be firm and snow white. Rinse and season fillets well with Kosher salt and roasted black pepper. Set on paper towels until ready to bake.

Generously coat roasting pan with unsalted butter. Place halibut fillets in pan. Top each fillet with a knob of butter. Bake halibut in oven until just firm to the touch for approximately 8-10 minutes. Do not over cook or fillets will be dry.

Poached Baby Leeks

8	Leeks	8
	Butter, olive oil, fish or vegetable stock	
to taste	Kosher salt	to taste
to taste	Roasted black pepper	to taste

Clean leeks well to remove any excess sand. Trim each leek in 3 inch (75 mm) pieces and cook gently in butter, good olive oil, fish or vegetable stock for approximately 8-10 minutes. Leeks should be nice and tender and not stringy. Remove leeks and drain well before lightly seasoning. Set aside and keep warm until serving.

Chanterelle Ragout

2 strips	Maple or double smoked bacon	2 strips
1 cup	Chanterelle mushrooms	250 ml
1/4 cup	Dry vermouth	50 ml
2 cloves	Garlic, chopped	2 cloves
1 cup	Heavy cream	250 ml
to taste	Kosher salt	to taste
to taste	Roasted black pepper	to taste
1/2	Lemon	1/2
4	Fresh basil leaves, large	4
2	Roma tomatoes, seeded, peeled and 1/4 inch (5 mm) dice	2

Slice bacon into thin strips. Render in a heavy saucepan until slightly crisp. Remove bacon and set aside. Cool bacon drippings slightly and sauté chanterelles until light and golden (do not overcook as chanterelles tend to become bitter). Add garlic and bacon to chanterelles. Remove from heat and drain off excess fat. Add dry vermouth and reduce by half. Add heavy cream and continue to reduce by one third. Adjust seasoning with salt and pepper. A light squeeze of lemon is optional.

Add chopped basil and lightly stir, bringing mixture to a simmer. Remove from heat and using a third of the sauce, blend with a stick blender until light and foamy. Add diced Roma tomatoes. Add the balance of the sauce to the ragout and use the foam for garnishing the dish.

Assembly: Assemble the dish by plating with a bed of leeks, followed by chanterelle ragout and topped with the halibut fillet. Garnish with sauce of choice.

Wine suggestion: CedarCreek Estate Winery Platinum Reserve Chardonnay, Okanagan Valley, 2000.

Scott Baechler, Executive Chef
Diva at the Met

Szechuan-Style Pan Fried Prawns
with Spicy Tomato Sauce

Serves: 4

8 oz.	Fresh prawns 31/40 count, shelled	250 g
1	Egg white, lightly beaten	1
1 tsp.	Salt	5 ml
2 1/2 tsp.	Corn starch	12 ml
10 1/3 oz.	Vegetable oil	310 ml
1/3 cup	White onion, minced	75 ml
1 clove	Garlic, minced	1 clove
1 tsp.	Fresh ginger, minced	5 ml
1–2 tsp.	Chinese chili sauce	5–10 ml
2 tbsp.	Tomato ketchup	30 ml
2 tsp.	Sugar	10 ml
2	Optional: small dried Szechuan peppers, minced	2
1 1/2 tsp.	Cold water	7 ml
	Cucumber and lemon slices for garnish	

Devein prawns and leave whole; marinate for 15 minutes in the egg white and 1/2 tsp. salt until prawns absorb egg white. Add 1 tsp. (5 ml) corn starch and let stand 15 minutes. Heat 10 oz. (300 ml) of oil in a hot wok to 360°F (185°C). Deep-fry marinated prawns 2-3 minutes, keeping them separated with long chopsticks. Lift prawns out with a strainer and drain. Discard oil, wipe wok clean and add 2 tsp. (10 ml) oil to wok. Combine onion, garlic and ginger and stir-fry for 1 minute. Add chili sauce and ketchup, sugar, remaining salt and peppers (if using). Return prawns to wok, heat through 30 seconds, tossing and thicken sauce with 1 1/2 tsp. corn starch and cold water for about 1 minute. Serve with steamed rice and garnish with fresh cucumber and lemon slices.

Alan Liu, Head Chef
Kirin Mandarin Restaurant

Honey and Ginger Beef

Serves: 4

"Ta Chi Mut" (it taste like honey) was the proclamation when this dish was served to the Empress by the Head Chef during the Ching Dynasty 100 years ago. We agree!

8 oz.	Beef tenderloin	250 g
2 tbsp.	Hoisin sauce	60 ml
1 tsp.	Corn starch	5 ml
10 1/2 oz.	Vegetable oil	315 ml
3 cloves	Garlic, minced	3 cloves
4 slices	Ginger, thinly sliced and minced	4 slices
1	Scallion, white part only, julienned	1
2 tbsp.	Honey	30 ml
1 tbsp.	Dark soya sauce	15 ml
	Fresh Chinese parsley sprigs for garnish	
	Steamed Chinese buns	

Slice beef paper thin, across the grain; marinate 15 minutes with hoisin sauce and corn starch.

Meanwhile heat 10 oz. (300 ml) of oil in a wok to 360°F (185°C). Deep-fry marinated beef for 1 minute, lift out at once with a strainer and set aside to drain. Discard oil, wipe wok clean and add 1 tbsp. (15 ml) oil to wok and heat. In separate bowl combine garlic, ginger, scallion and then stir-fry for 1 minute. Add honey and soya sauce, cook 15 seconds and return drained beef to wok. Stir-fry 1 minute until beef is glazed. Serve on a platter, garnished with sprigs of Chinese parsley and accompany with warm steamed buns.

Alan Liu, Head Chef
Kirin Mandarin Restaurant

Anatra Melata
Roasted Duck Breast with
Maple and Apple Succo

Serves: 4

4	Muscovy duck breasts	4
1/4 cup	Brandy	50 ml
1/2 cup	Maple syrup	125 ml
1	Granny smith apple, cored and sliced	1
1 cup	Chicken stock	250 ml
to taste	Salt and cracked pepper	to taste
1/4 cup	Almonds, sliced and toasted	50 ml

Preheat oven to 350°F (180°C). Score the skin side of the duck. Place duck skin side down in a dry pan on medium heat. Render skin until it's crispy and golden. Turn breasts over and place skinless side down. Place pan in oven and roast for 10 minutes until medium-done. Remove duck breast from oven and set aside. De-glaze pan with brandy and maple syrup. Add sliced apple and chicken stock and reduce to sauce consistency. Season to taste with salt and cracked pepper. Slice duck breasts and fan out onto serving plates. Spoon sauce over duck and sprinkle with almonds.

Serving suggestions: Serve with polenta, or mashed or roast potatoes.

Bradford Ellis, Executive Chef
Quattro on Fourth

Coelho em Vinha-d'alho
(Braised Rabbit)

Serves: 4

1	Rabbit, cut into pieces	1
3 cloves	Garlic	3 cloves
1 tsp.	Salt	5 ml
4 slices	Country bread	4 slices
2	Medium onions, thinly sliced	2
6 slices	Bacon	6 slices
2 tbsp.	Olive oil	30 ml
5 oz.	Port wine	150 ml

Combine salt and garlic, blend into a paste, and coat the rabbit. Layer ovenware dish with bread, rabbit pieces, onion slices, and bacon strips and drizzle with olive oil. Braise in oven at 375°F (190°C) for 45 minutes or until tender; add port and continue to cook for 15 minutes.

Manuel Ferreira, Chef/Owner
Le Gavroche

Grilled Fillet of Wild Salmon,
Pickled Blueberries, Frisée Lettuce with a Grainy Mustard Vinaigrette and Crème Fraîche

Serves: 4

4 x 6 oz.	Wild salmon fillet boneless and skin removed	4 x 180 g
to taste	Fine sea salt and cracked black pepper	to taste
1/2 cup	Vegetable oil	100 ml
2 heads	Frisée lettuce	2 heads

Pickled Blueberries

2 lbs.	Blueberries, fresh or frozen	900 g
1 cup	Maple syrup	250 ml
3/4 cup	Sherry vinegar	175 ml
1 tsp.	Coriander seeds	5 ml
1 tsp.	Brown mustard seeds	5 ml

Pour maple syrup into a heavy bottomed pan and cook over high heat until it begins to caramelize, approximately 7-8 minutes. Remove from heat and carefully add the sherry vinegar. Over high heat, in a small pan, heat the coriander and mustard seeds together until they turn a few shades darker, approximately 3-4 minutes. Add the seeds to the maple syrup mixture. Purée 4 oz. (100 g) of the blueberries and add this as well as the remaining whole blueberries. Stir mixture well.

Grainy Mustard Vinaigrette

1	Egg yolk	1
1 oz.	Shallots	25 g
1 tsp.	Garlic	6 g
2 tbsp.	Grainy mustard	35 g
1/3 cup	Sherry vinegar	75 ml
1 cup	Hazelnut oil	250 ml
1 cup	Vegetable oil	250 ml
to taste	Fine sea salt and ground white pepper	to taste

Combine egg yolk, shallots, garlic, mustard and vinegar in a blender or food processor. Purée until smooth. With blender on high speed, drizzle the oils (alternate between them) until a smooth dressing is achieved. Season with salt and white pepper to taste

Crème Fraîche (make ahead)

2/3 cup	Buttermilk, 3.25%	150 ml
300 ml	Whipping cream, 36 %	300 ml

Combine the buttermilk and whipping cream and mix well. Pour into a sterile earthenware container or mason jar (do not use a metallic container). Cover loosely with plastic wrap and place in a warm area for 48 hours. After 48 hours, cover tightly and refrigerate.

Assembly

Preheat outdoor barbeque or stove top grill on highest setting. Season salmon fillets with sea salt and pepper. Dip a section of a clean, dry cloth into the vegetable oil, and carefully rub the barbeque or indoor grill with it (this will prevent the salmon fillets from sticking).

Carefully place the salmon fillets flesh side down. Wait 2 minutes, lift and turn 45 degrees to produce crossed grill marks. Wait an additional 2 minutes and flip the salmon fillet. A further 2 minutes cooking time should cook to medium rare. Remove and keep warm.

Divide the washed and dried frisée into four equal portions and toss with enough of the grainy mustard vinaigrette to coat. Spoon approximately 1/3 cup (75 ml) of the pickled blueberries onto the centre of a serving plate. Place the dressed frisée atop. Next, place the salmon fillet on the frisée. Top with a heaping tablespoon of the crème fraîche, garnish as desired, and serve.

Dino Gazzola, Executive Chef
Bridges Restaurant

Fettucine Tartufate
with Portabella Mushrooms and Truffle

Serves: 4

1/4 cup	Truffle oil	50 ml
1	Shallot, chopped	1
3 cloves	Garlic, chopped	3 cloves
2	Portabella mushrooms, thinly sliced and no stems	2
1/4 cup	Dry porcini mushrooms, soaked (just enough water to cover), reserve water	50 ml
2 cups	Cream, 35%	500 ml
2 tbsp.	Truffle paste	30 ml
to taste	Salt and pepper	to taste
2 tbsp.	Fresh sage, chopped	30 ml

In a medium-large sauce pan sauté truffle oil, shallot and garlic until soft. Add sliced portabellas and sauté until soft. Add porcini water and chopped porcinis. Add cream and reduce. Add truffle paste, salt, pepper and sage.

Serving suggestion: Serve with cooked pasta and Reggiano cheese.

Bradford Ellis, Executive Chef
Quattro on Fourth

Pad Kee Maow
(Noodle Stir-fry)

Serves: 2

1/2 package	Medium Rice noodles	1/2 package
5 tbsp.	Oil	75 ml
1 tsp.	Garlic, chopped	5 ml
1/4 cup	Chicken, chopped	50 ml
1/4 cup	Shrimp, chopped	50 ml
1 tbsp.	Shallots, chopped	15 ml
1 tbsp	Oyster sauce	15 ml
1 tbsp.	Sugar	15 ml
1 tbsp	Light soya sauce	15 ml
1 tbsp.	Fish sauce	15 ml
1/2 tsp.	Dried chili, ground	2 ml
1 tbsp.	Chopped mixed red and green peppers	15 ml
1/3 cup	Fresh Thai basil leaves (available at Asian stores)	75 ml
3 tbsp.	Chicken stock	45 ml
1	Egg, beaten	1
1/4 cup	Bean sprouts Handful of fresh bean sprouts and more Thai basil for garnish	50 ml

Soak the noodles in water for about 15 minutes, then drain.In a high heat wok, add the oil, garlic and chicken and stir until cooked. Add noodles and stir-fry until noodles are soft. Reduce heat to medium.

Add the remaining ingredients (except the bean sprouts) and stir-fry until cooked through. Now add the bean sprouts. Garnish with Thai basil.

Siriwan (Grace) Rerksuttisiridach, Executive Chef/Owner
Simply Thai Restaurant

Pesto Salmon

Serves: 2

Salmon

2 x 6 oz.	Salmon fillets	2 x 170 g
5 tbsp.	Olive oil	75 ml
to taste	Salt and white pepper	to taste

Prepare a hot charcoal or wood fire in a covered grill. Brush the salmon all over with olive oil and season to taste with salt and pepper. Grill the salmon, turning once and basting occasionally with the oil for 6–10 minutes total cooking time, depending on thickness of salmon. Place the salmon on a warm plate and spoon Pesto Sauce over it.

Pesto Sauce

1/4 cup	Olive oil	50 ml
1/2 cup	Pine nuts, ground	100 ml
1/4 cup	Garlic, puréed	50 ml
4 oz.	Fresh basil, finely chopped	120 g
1/4 cup	Parmesan cheese, grated	50 ml
to taste	Salt and pepper	to taste
4 tbsp.	Cream	60 ml

Mix all ingredients, except cream, in a blender. Put the pesto mixture in a small frying pan, add cream, simmer for 10 minutes and set aside in a warm place.

Serving suggestion: Serve with garlic mashed potatoes, baby carrots, and steamed asparagus or green beans.

Richard Taoukil, Executive Chef
Prospect Point Restaurant

Steamed Salmon in Banana Leaf

Serves: 4

The banana leaf imparts a very distinct flavour which steaming intensifies. If you can't find banana leaf, use spinach, endive, lettuce or even green grape leaves. Cooking parchment also works.

1/2 cup	Milk	125 ml
1 tsp.	Dried coconut, unsweetened, fine	5 ml
1/4 cup	Fresh mint, chopped	50 ml
4 cloves	Garlic, crushed	4 cloves
1 tsp.	Ground cumin	5 ml
4	Green chilies, crushed or to taste	4
2 tsp.	Lemon juice	10 ml
1 1/2 lb.	Salmon, cod, halibut or red snapper cut into 4 pieces	750 g
2	Banana leaves, halved	2
1/2 tsp.	Salt	2 ml
1/2 tsp.	Pepper	2 ml
3/4 cup	Water	175 ml
1/4 cup	Vinegar	50 ml
8	Dried curry leaves or 4 bay leaves	8

Combine milk, coconut, mint, garlic, cumin, green chilies and lemon juice. Set aside for 10 minutes. Dry fish on paper towel. Place each piece in centre of banana leaf. Sprinkle with salt and pepper, let sit for 5 minutes. Spoon coconut mixture over fish. Fold leaf and tie with kitchen string. If you are using parchment paper, make sure the package encloses the fish completely but leaves enough space for the steam to infuse its aroma. Heat water with vinegar and curry leaves in a pot large enough to hold vegetable steamer. Bring water to boil. Put fish packets in steamer over water and steam covered for 15 minutes. Serve immediately. If using other edible leaves for wrapping, be sure you have enough to wrap 4 servings.

Serving suggestions: Serve with Aaloo Gobi, (page 24) and steamed rice.

Krishna Jamal, Executive Chef
Rubina Tandoori

Sockeye Salmon Fillet

with Bocconcini Herb Crust, Saffron Risotto and Barbera Wine Jus

Serves: 2

| 2 x 7 oz. | Salmon fillets, centre cut | 2 x 200 g |
| | Vegetable oil for sautéing | |

Remove skin and fat. Season and set aside.

Bocconcini Herb Crust

7 oz.	Bocconcini cheese	200 g
to taste	Fresh herbs; thyme, rosemary, chive, sage or basil	to taste
to taste	Black pepper	to taste

Place cheese between layers of paper towel and set aside. While cheese is drying, pick through herbs removing stems. Finely chop herbs. Cut the cheese into 1/2 inch (1 cm) cubes. Combine herbs and cheese, kneading the mixture with your hands. Finish with freshly ground black pepper. Set aside.

Saffron Risotto

3 tbsp.	Butter	45 ml
1/2	Onion, medium, finely diced	1/2
3-4	Garlic cloves, minced	3-4
1 1/2 cups	Arborio rice	375 ml
15-20 threads	Saffron	15-20 threads
4-5 cups	Chicken stock	1-1.2 litres
1/4 cup	Parmesan **or** asiago cheese, grated	50 ml
3 tbsp.	Butter	45 ml
to taste	Salt and white pepper	to taste

Melt butter in a heavy-bottomed sauce pan on medium-low heat. Sweat the onion, without browning, until soft and translucent. Add garlic. After a few minutes turn down heat and add rice. Gently sauté without colouring. After 2-3 minutes add saffron, stir, and add enough heated stock to cover rice by a few centimetres. Stir the risotto frequently to prevent sticking. As the rice begins to absorb the stock (texture of porridge) add another half cup of stock and stir again. Repeat, stirring often for about 30-40 minutes. It will be done (*al dente*) when the rice is soft with a slight firmness in the centre. When served, it should not run nor keep it's shape or hold a peak. Finish by adding grated cheese, butter, salt and pepper. Serve immediately or set it on lowest possible heat for up to 20 minutes.

Barbera Wine Jus

	Olive oil as needed	
4-5	Shallots, medium, thinly sliced	4-5
5 cloves	Garlic, minced	5 cloves
1 tbsp.	Sugar	15 ml
1 1/2 cup	Red wine, Barbera or another medium-bodied, fruity wine	375 ml
3 sprigs	Fresh thyme	3 sprigs
1 sprig	Fresh rosemary	1 sprig
1	Bay leaf	1
3	Peppercorns	3
3 cups	Veal stock	750 ml
1 1/2 oz.	Butter, cold, cubed	40 g

This is a reduction. Preheat a heavy-bottomed pot over medium-high heat, generously coat the bottom of the pot with olive oil. Just before the olive oil "smokes", add shallots. Cook until they start to brown. Turn down heat and add garlic — do not burn. Cook for a few minutes adding sugar. When it has dissolved and is beginning to caramelize, deglaze the pan with red wine. Add herbs, bay leaf and peppercorns and reduce until almost dry. Add the veal stock and reduce, simmering to 1 1/4 cup (300 ml). Skim off any fat or foam that rises to the surface. The sauce should coat the back of a spoon when you remove it from the heat. Whisk in the butter to thicken and smooth it. Adjust seasoning.

Assembly: Preheat oven to 450°F (230°C). Preheat a sauté pan on high heat and add vegetable oil generously. When the oil reaches smoking point, add salmon fillets, gently shaking it to prevent sticking. Make sure the pan is very hot or the salmon will not release. Once it has a golden crust, place in a pan seared side up and cover with bocconcini crust. Finish in the oven until cheese is melted and the fish is done. Place risotto on the plate, top with crusted salmon and drizzle sauce over the dish.

Sylvain Cuerrier, Executive Chef
The Observatory Restaurant at Grouse Mountain

Yin-Yang Four Way Salmon

Serves: 4-6

This dish incorporates four different recipes in one meal.

Salmon Tartare with Asian Flavours

8 oz.	Salmon, minced and trimmed	250 g
1 tsp.	Rice wine or sake	5 ml
1 tbsp.	Fresh ginger, minced	15 ml
1 tsp.	Shallots, minced	5 ml
1 1/2 tbsp.	Scallion, minced	23 ml
1 tsp.	Soya sauce	5 ml
1 tsp.	Sesame oil	5 ml
to taste	Salt and pepper	to taste

Combine everything together in a non-reactive bowl. Chill in the refrigerator. Serve on just about anything; rice crackers, toast points, etc.

Seared Salmon with Pine Nut Crust

8 oz.	Salmon	250 g
1 cup	Dry bread	250 ml
1/2 cup	Pine nuts, toasted	125 ml
1 tbsp.	Kosher salt	15 ml
1 tsp.	Butter, cold	5 ml
	Fresh chives or scallions	

Using a food processor, pulse the bread and pine nuts together. Mix the butter into the bread and nuts and add salt to taste. Pre-sear the fish slightly, top with the crust and bake at 450°F (230°C) for 6 minutes or until desired temperature. Garnish with chive sticks or scallions and a drizzle of black vinegar.

Teriyaki Glazed Salmon

8 oz.	Salmon	250 g
1 cup	Soya sauce	250 ml
1 cup	Brown sugar	250 ml
1 tbsp.	Fresh ginger, minced	15 ml
6-7 cloves	Garlic, minced	6-7 cloves

Place everything except the salmon in a pot and reduce to about 1/3 cup (75 ml). This takes about 15 minutes. Grill the salmon on the BBQ or in a frying pan and just before the fish has finished cooking to your liking, brush on the glaze.

Tempura Salmon

8 oz.	Salmon	250 g
1/2 cup	Flour	125 g
1/2 cup	Corn Starch	125 g
1/4 cup	Sake	50 ml
1/4 cup	Cold water	50 ml
2 tsp.	Baking Soda	10 ml
	Vegetable oil for frying	

Cut the salmon in half. Heat vegetable oil in a deep pan or deep fryer to 340-350°F (175-180°C). Combine all ingredients except salmon in a non-reactive metal bowl and stir together lightly. Do not over mix the batter. Lightly dip salmon in the batter and immediately fry the pieces until brown along the edges. Turn over several times during cooking.

Serving suggestion: Arrange all four salmon dishes on one large serving platter and allow everyone to sample.

Lynda Larouche
The Teahouse Restaurant in Stanley Park at Ferguson Point

British Columbian
Halibut Congee
with Chinese Silverfish Crackers

Serves: 4

Chinese Silverfish Crackers

4 cups	All purpose flour	1 kg
4 cups	Panko*	1 kg
1 cup	Water	250 ml
1 tbsp.	Salt	15 ml
2 tbsp.	Baking powder	30 ml
1 lb.	Silverfish **, roughly chopped	500 g

To make the crackers, combine flour, panko, water, salt, baking powder and roughly chopped silverfish in medium sized mixing bowl. Work into fairly stiff dough. Add a little more flour if needed. Roll dough out onto parchment paper to 1/8 inch (3 mm) thickness. Cut into 3 x 3 inch (8 x 8 cm) squares.

* Flakey Japanese bread crumbs
** Tiny fish found at Chinese supermarket in either fresh or frozen section.

Congee

3/4 cup	Jasmine rice (not rinsed)	175 ml
2 cups	Fish stock	500 ml
1 1/2 tbsp.	Rice wine vinegar	22 ml
1 1/2 tbsp.	Mirin (sweet red wine)	22 ml
2	Lemons, juice and zest	2
1 tsp.	Fresh ginger, finely minced	5 ml
1 lb.	Halibut fillet, roughly chopped	450 g
to taste	Salt	to taste
4 tbsp.	Fresh cilantro, finely chopped	60 ml
1 cup	Pea shoots	250 ml
1/2 cup	Scallions, julienned	125 ml
2 cups	Vegetable oil	500 ml

Combine rice, fish stock, rice wine vinegar, mirin, lemon juice and zest, ginger and halibut in heavy-bottom pot. Cook on medium heat until the mixture becomes cloudy and slightly thickened. Lower heat and adjust seasoning with salt and lemon juice. It is ready when it has the consistency of runny porridge. Just before serving, add the chopped cilantro.

On another burner at the same time, heat the vegetable oil until it's just starting to smoke. Place crackers in one at a time, frying on both sides until golden brown. Remove from oil and season with salt. Garnish the congee with pea shoots, scallions, and fish crackers (stand the crackers on end).

Stuart Irving, Chef
Wild Rice

Charred Beef Tenderloin
with Zong Bao Triangles

Serves: 4

12-14oz	Beef tenderloin, cleaned	340-400 g

Marinade

1 cup	Fah Koo mushrooms, ground **or** dried Chinese Shitake*	250 ml
1 tsp.	Salt	5 ml
1 tsp.	Fresh garlic, finely chopped	5 ml
1 tsp.	Shallot, finely chopped	5 ml
1 tsp.	Fresh ginger, finely chopped	5 ml
1 tbsp.	Vegetable oil	15 ml

Cut beef tenderloin into 4 steaks, and marinate with the ground mushroom, salt, garlic, shallot, ginger, and vegetable oil.

*If you are using dried mushrooms cut them small and run them through a food processor or a coffee grinder.

Sauces

1/3 cup	Kecap manis (sweet soy)	75 ml
1 tbsp.	Mirin (sweet rice wine)	15 ml
1 tbsp.	Tamarind extract	15 ml
1/3 cup	Hoi Sin sauce	75 ml
1 tbsp.	Rice wine vinegar	15 ml
4 cups	Vegetable oil	900 ml

In a small bowl, whisk together the kecap manis, mirin and tamarind extract. In another small bowl, whisk together the hoi sin and rice wine vinegar. Set both aside

Zong Bao Triangles

4 cups	Sticky or sushi rice	900 ml
5 cups	Water	1.2 L
2 tbsp.	Salt	30 ml
2 tbsp.	Sugar	30 ml

WILD RICE

3	Portabello mushroom caps, large	3
8	Shitake mushroom caps	8
4 cups	Spinach leaves, washed, stemless	900 ml
2 cups	Cloud ear mushrooms	500 ml
	(reconstitute with boiling water)	
2 oz.	White wine or chicken stock	55 ml
to taste	Salt	to taste

Thoroughly rinse the sticky/sushi rice twice in a heavy-bottomed sauce pan. Pour off water. Add water, salt and sugar. Cover and place on medium high heat until it comes to a boil. Turn to low heat immediately and cook gently for about 20 minutes or until all liquid is absorbed. Spread rice over parchment-lined cookie sheet to an even 1 inch (2.5 cm) thickness and let cool completely. When cooled to room temperature place in refrigerator for 1-2 hours.

Cut portabello caps into 1 inch (2.5 cm) slices. Cut shitake caps the same way. Prepare separately spinach and portabello and cloud ear mushrooms. Set aside. Cut the refrigerated rice into 4 x 4 inch (10 x 10 cm) squares, and then cut diagonally to create triangles. Heat vegetable oil until it is just starting to smoke. Place the triangles, carefully, two at a time, and fry until golden brown on both sides. When all the triangles are done, place on cookie tray, to be re-heated or kept warm in the oven for service.

Assembly: Grill the steaks to desired temperature. At the same time sauté the portabello and shitake mushrooms on the stove. Add the cloud ears, white wine or chicken stock and salt. When done, add the spinach on top to wilt. On each warm triangle, lay a portion of the spinach/mushroom mixture along with a few slices of the steak. Drizzle alternately with the kecap and hoi sin sauce. Stack the triangles three high at most.

Serving suggestions: An Australian Shiraz, aged at least 2 years is a fine accompaniment. A side dish of grilled bok choy lightly brushed with soy and ginger is a perfect companion dish.

Stuart Irving, Chef
Wild Rice

Oyster Stew
with Leeks and White Vermouth

Serves: 4

2 tbsp.	Butter	30 ml
2	Medium leek, thinly sliced white part only	1
12	Large oysters, fresh shucked, with juices	12
1/2 cup	White vermouth	125 ml
1 tbsp.	Lemon zest	15 ml
1/2 cup	Whipping cream	125 ml
to taste	Salt and black pepper, freshly ground	to taste
1/4 cup	Fresh chives, chopped	60 ml

Melt butter in a frying pan on medium heat. Sauté leek until softened, 2-3 minutes. Add oysters and their juices; cook until they just begin to plump up, about 1 minute. Deglaze the pan by adding vermouth and stirring to loosen the browned bits on the bottom. Add lemon zest and whipping cream. Bring to a boil on medium heat, then turn down to medium-low; simmer, uncovered, until oysters are slightly firm to the touch, about 5 minutes. Season with salt and pepper.

You can vary the sauce by allowing the cream to reduce to the thickness that you prefer. This offers a great deal of flexibility in how the dish is served. A thinner sauce turns this dish into excellent, rich soup: a meal in itself. A slightly thicker sauce makes the stew a delicious starter or even a lunch dish if you serve it ladled over a piece of toast and sprinkle with a small amount of freshly grated Parmesan cheese.

Assembly: Ladle three oysters and some sauce into each warmed soup bowl and top with some of the cooked leek. Sprinkle with chopped chives.

Dennis Green, Executive Chef
Bishop's

Honey Mustard Free-Range Chicken Breast

Serves: 6

Chef Dennis Green developed this marinade to cook the organic chickens from local farmer Thomas Reid. We've found that organic or free-range chickens generally have a better flavour. The marinade leaves the chicken really tender while the honey makes the skin golden brown and crispy. This dish may be served warm or cold — perfect for a picnic.

1/2 cup	Dry white wine	125 ml
1/4 cup	Honey	60 ml
1/2 cup	Grainy mustard	125 ml
1/2 cup	Vegetable oil	125 ml
pinch	Black pepper, freshly ground	pinch
6	Chicken breast halves	6
	or 1 whole cut-up chicken	
	Sprigs of fresh thyme for garnish	

Combine white wine and honey in a small saucepan on medium heat and bring to a boil. Whisk in mustard, vegetable oil and pepper until well mixed, then allow to cool. Place chicken in a shallow pan and pour marinade over it. Cover and marinate overnight in the refrigerator.

Preheat the oven to 400°F (200°C) and line a shallow baking pan with parchment paper.

Remove chicken from marinade and place in the prepared baking pan. Bake until chicken is golden brown in colour and cooked, approximately 20 to 30 minutes. Check for doneness with a meat thermometer; the internal temperature should read 190°F (85°C). Allow it to rest for 5 minutes before serving.

Assembly: Either leave the chicken breasts (or cut-up pieces) whole or carve them diagonally and arrange slices on warmed plates. Garnish with a sprig of thyme.

Dennis Green, Executive Chef
Bishop's

Kunsei Gindara in Parchment
(Smoked Sablefish)

Serves: 4

1 lb.	Smoked sablefish fillets, skinned, cut into 4 oz. (110 g) pieces	450 g
1/4 cup	Dashi (Bonito stock) **or** chicken **or** fish stock	50 ml
1 tbsp.	Light shoyu or soya sauce	15 ml
1 tbsp.	Mirin sauce	15 ml
1	Pine **or** King mushroom, cleaned, trimmed, peeled and cut lengthwise into 1/8 inch (3 mm) slices. Shitake **or** emoki mushrooms may be substituted.	1
4 stalks	Asparagus, trimmed	4 stalks
1	Mango, under-ripe, peeled, julienned (1/2 x 1/2 x 3 1/2 inch, or 12 mm x 12 mm x 90 mm)	1
	Vegetable oil	
4 sheets	Parchment paper	4 sheets
garnish	Pine needles, sudachi (Japanese citrus)	garnish

To double fillet the fish for stuffing, place fillet flesh side up on a cutting board with the grain of the fish running parallel to the top edge of the board. Starting on one side of the fillet, at a point about one third of the way down, make the first horizontal butterfly cut across the fillet stopping about 1/3 inch (8 mm) before reaching the opposite edge. Be careful not to cut through the whole fillet. From the end of this first cut, make a second butterfly cut going the opposite direction from the first, stopping, as with the first cut before cutting through the fish. As a result, each fillet should open up like a two-fold brochure into one long piece, about a third of the thickness of the original. Set the fillets aside.

Preheat oven to 450°F (230°C).

In a saucepan over medium heat, mix together the dashi, shoyu and mirin. Add the mushrooms and gently cook for 2-3 minutes or until slightly soft. Do not over-cook. Strain, reserving the marinade in

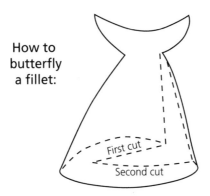

How to butterfly a fillet:

First cut

Second cut

another saucepan and setting aside the mushrooms to cool. Cut the asparagus stalks in half. Heat up the marinade over medium heat and blanch the stalks for 1 to 2 minutes or until they are slightly soft but are still firm. Remove from heat and set aside to cool. Place a sheet of parchment paper on a clean surface. Lightly brush the centre area of the paper where the fish will be placed with oil. To assemble, place a sablefish fillet on a clean surface and extend out the butterflied layers. Place a piece of asparagus, mango and a quarter of the mushrooms in the middle of the filet. Roll up and place the cut side facing down onto the middle of the oiled parchment paper.

Bring together the top and bottom ends of the parchment paper making a single tight fold, as if you were gift wrapping a parcel. Fold down the ends and crease the excess paper underneath the parcel. This can also be done with aluminum foil. Place the parcels onto a baking sheet and place into the middle of a preheated oven and bake for 10 minutes. To serve, place parcels onto a serving plate and garnish with pine needles and a half sudachi.

Hidekazu Tojo, Executive Chef/Owner
Tojo's

Grilled Sablefish, Brandade of Smoked Black Cod
and Creamed Spinach

Serves: 4

Brandade of Smoked Black Cod

1 1/2 lbs.	Yukon gold potatoes	700 g
1 1/2 lbs.	Smoked black cod	700 g
2 cups	Milk	500 ml
1/2 cup	Extra virgin olive oil	125 ml
1 tbsp.	Truffle oil	15 ml
1 clove	Garlic, chopped	1 clove
to taste	Salt and pepper	to taste
to taste	Parsley, chopped	to taste

Boil and peel potatoes and pass through a ricer or food mill. Reserve potatoes warm. Poach smoked cod in milk for approximately 10 minutes, until cooked. Heat half of the olive oil in a heavy pot, add cod, mix to break up. Add potatoes; mix well, adding chopped garlic, salt and pepper, the rest of the olive oil and finally the chopped parsley.

Creamed Spinach

1/2 lb.	Baby spinach leaves, stemless	225 g
1 tsp.	Butter	5 ml
1/2	Shallot	1/2
1 clove	Garlic, chopped	1 clove
1 cup	Cream	250 ml
to taste	Salt, pepper and nutmeg	to taste

Sweat baby spinach with butter over moderate heat until wilted. Add shallot and garlic. Add cream and reduce to a consistency that coats the back of a spoon. Season with salt, pepper and nutmeg.

Grilled Sablefish

4 x 5 oz.	Sablefish pieces	4 x 140 g	
1 tsp.	Olive oil	5 ml	
to taste	Salt and pepper	to taste	

Season and rub sablefish with the olive oil. Place on a hot BBQ and cook approximately 2-3 minutes on each side.

Assembly: Place a ring of creamed spinach on a plate. Top with the Brandade of Smoked Black Cod and finally the Grilled Sablefish. Garnish with fresh baby greens.

Bradley Miller, Chef
Pastis

Salmon with Maple Glaze

Serves: 4

4 x 6 oz.	Salmon fillets	4 x 170 g
to taste	Salt and pepper	to taste
4	Dried corn husks, soaked in water overnight (optional)	4

Season the salmon with salt and pepper and wrap in the cornhusks. Either grill or bake at 350°F (180°C) for 10-15 minutes until just cooked through. You don't have to use the corn husks. The salmon is delicious just with the sauce.

Maple Glaze

2 tbsp.	Water	30 ml
1/2 cup	Brown sugar	125 ml
1 tbsp.	White wine vinegar	15 ml
1/4 tsp.	Salt	1 ml
1/2 cup	Maple syrup	125 ml
3/4 cup	Whipping cream	175 ml
1 tbsp.	Cider vinegar	15 ml

Combine water and sugar in a large pot, to prevent it from boiling over. Bring to a boil, add the vinegars, salt and maple syrup. Add the whipping cream and boil for 3-5 minutes until the sauce thickens slightly. Remove from heat.

To serve: Open corn husks and place salmon in the centre of a plate. Drizzle with Maple Glaze. Accompany with fresh corn on the cob or another fresh steamed vegetable.

Wine suggestion: Pinot Gris goes well with this dish.

Karen Barnaby, Executive Chef
The Fish House in Stanley Park

Char Kway Teow
(Rice Noodles)

Serves: 8

1 tbsp.	Oil	15 ml
2 cloves	Garlic, finely chopped	2 cloves
2	Eggs, beaten	2
pinch	Salt	
6-8	Large shrimp, peeled	6-8
2	Chinese sausages, cut into pieces	2
16-20	Clam, shells discarded	16-20
1 tbsp.	Chili paste	15 ml
1 lb.	Rice-flour noodles (Kway Teow), soaked in warm water for 10 minutes.	450 g
1/2 cup	Chopped garlic chives	125 ml
2 cups	Bean sprouts	500 ml
pinch	Salt	pinch
2 tbsp.	Kecap Manis*	30 ml
4 tbsp.	Light soya sauce	60 ml

Heat the oil in the wok. Sauté the garlic for a few seconds, then add egg, shrimp, Chinese sausage and clam meat. Stir for a few moments, then add chili paste. Add drained noodles. Stir-fry for a few minutes or until noodles turn slightly yellow, then add chives and bean sprouts. Season with salt, kicap manis and soya sauce. Continue to stir-fry until the noodles are thoroughly heated. Serve immediately.

* Black sweet soya sauce

Calvin Chong, Chef/Owner
Banana Leaf Malaysian Restaurant

Singapore Chili Crab

Serves: 6

2 lbs.	Fresh crabs, cleaned and cut	900 g
	Oil for deep-frying	
1/2 cup	Cooking oil for stir fry	125 ml
10 cloves	Garlic, finely chopped	10 cloves
2 inches	Fresh ginger, roughly chopped	5 cm
3	Red chilies, finely chopped	3
1 tbsp.	Chili sauce	15 ml
1/2 cup	Tomato sauce	125 ml
1 tbsp.	Sugar	15 ml
1 tbsp.	Light soya sauce	15 ml
1 tbsp.	Sesame oil	15 ml
1 cup	Chicken stock	250 ml
1 tbsp.	Corn flour, mixed with	15 ml
	3 tbsp (45 ml) water	
1	Egg, lightly beaten	1
to taste	Salt and pepper	to taste
1	Green onion, sliced	1

Deep-fry the crabs in hot oil just until bright red. Remove and set aside. Pour out the oil and put 1/2 cup fresh oil in the wok. Heat and add garlic, ginger and chilies. Stir until fragrant then add chili sauce, tomato sauce, sugar, soy sauce and sesame oil. Simmer for 1 minute then season to taste with salt and pepper. Add the fried crab and stir to coat well with sauce. Add the chicken stock and cook over high heat for 3 minutes. Stir thoroughly and thicken with corn flour and egg. Season to taste with salt and pepper, and sprinkle with green onions.

To serve: Serve with steamed rice.

Calvin Chong, Chef/Owner
Banana Leaf Malaysian Restaurant

Salmon with Blueberry Sauce

Serves: 1

4 oz.	Salmon, your preference	125 g
3 oz.	Wild rice, cooked	85 g
2 oz.	Blueberry sauce (see below)	55 g
3 oz.	Seasonal vegetables, cooked to your liking	85 g
1 sprig	Fresh dill	1 sprig

Preheat oven to 400°F (200°C). Bake salmon for 7-9 minutes until cooked through. Place on top of rice in the centre of a plate with vegetables beside. Garnish with dill.

Blueberry Sauce

Serves: 4

1 lb.	Fresh blueberries if available	450 g
1 cup	White sugar	250 ml
5	Limes, zest	5
3	Limes, juice	3
1/4 cup	Red wine vinegar	50 ml

Combine all ingredients and reduce until sauce is shiny and of a desired consistency.

Mark Jorundson, Chef
Rocky Mountaineer Railtours

Duo of Sesame Ahi Tuna
with Wasabi Risotto and Miso Shitake
Mushroom Cream Sauce and Spinach Gomae

Serves: 4

4 x 7 oz.	Ahi tuna	4 x 200 g
	Oil for frying	
1/2 cup each	Black and white sesame seeds	125 ml each
to garnish	Popcorn sprouts	to garnish

Pan-fry tuna in oil for 1-2 minutes, depending on the thickness. With the two different coloured sesame seeds, draw two parallel lines across the middle of each tuna steak.

Miso Shitake Mushroom Cream Sauce

2 tbsp.	Vegetable oil	30 ml
1/2 lb.	Shitake mushrooms, thinly sliced, stems removed	225 g
3/4 cup	Miso paste	175 ml
1/4 cup	White wine	50 g
4 1/3 cups	Whipping cream	1 litre
to taste	White pepper	to taste

Drizzle oil into a small saucepan at medium heat. Let the pan get hot and then add mushrooms. Sauté until translucent. Incorporate miso paste and stir until smooth. Pour in the wine and reduce for 30 seconds. Add whipping cream, let the mixture reach a boil and then turn off the heat. Add a pinch of white pepper.

Wasabi Sticky Rice Risotto

2/3 cup	Cooking oil	175 ml
2 tbsp.	White onion, finely diced	30 ml
2 cups	Japanese sticky rice	450 g
4-6 cups	Water	l-1.5 litres
1/4 cup	Light soya sauce	50 ml
1/4 cup	Wasabi powder	50 ml

Heat oil in a heavy saucepan on medium heat. Sauté onions until translucent. Add rice and stir for 1 minute. Combine water, soya sauce and wasabi powder and add to the rice 1/2 cup (125 ml) at a time, waiting for the liquid to be absorbed before continuing. Stir constantly. It will take about 20 minutes for the rice to be *al dente* (just slightly under cooked). Test frequently. Remove from the stove and spread the rice out on a baking sheet to cool. Fill individual moulds with cooled rice and reheat when ready to serve.

Sautéed Ginger Carrots

12 oz.	Carrots, julienned	350 g
2 tbsp.	Fresh ginger, minced	30 ml
1 tbsp.	Honey, unpasteurised	15 ml
to taste	Salt and pepper	to taste

Blanch carrots in boiling, salted water for 30 seconds. Strain. Sauté ginger at medium-high heat for 10-15 seconds. Add carrots and cook for another 30-40 seconds. Pour in the honey. Season to taste.

Spinach Gomae

8 oz.	Blanched spinach, refrigerated	250 g
1/4 cup	Soya sauce	50 ml
1/4 cup	Sesame oil	50 ml
6 tbsp.	Honey	80 ml

Whisk together all ingredients except the spinach. Set aside.

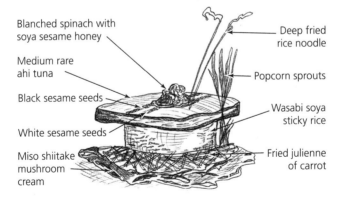

Blanched spinach with soya sesame honey

Medium rare ahi tuna

Black sesame seeds

White sesame seeds

Miso shiitake mushroom cream

Deep fried rice noodle

Popcorn sprouts

Wasabi soya sticky rice

Fried julienne of carrot

Assembly: In the middle of each of four plates, put a spoonful of Miso Shitake Mushroom Cream Sauce. Arrange Sautéed Ginger Carrots next and then top with reheated Wasabi Risotto. Place Tuna on top of risotto; garnish with Spinach Gomae and popcorn sprouts.

Dobrosav Kovacevic, Executive Chef
A Kettle of Fish

Double Cooked Angus Striploin
with Marinated Grilled Mushrooms, Corn Bread and Star Anise Sauce

Serves: 4

Bareback Corn Bread

Yield: 4 round breads

4	Eggs	4
3/4 cup	Vegetable oil	175 ml
1 cup	Cream cheese	250 ml
3/4 cup	Sour cream	175 ml
3/4 cup	Milk, warm	175 ml
3/4 cup	Flour, all purpose	175 ml
2 tbsp.	Baking powder	30 ml
1/2 tsp.	Salt	2 ml

Preheat oven to 350°F (180°C). Blend eggs and oil in a mixer at low speed. In another bowl blend cream cheese and sour cream by hand. Add milk to cheese mixture. Add cheese mixture to the oil and egg mixture. Mix. Add all other ingredients. Place on a greased baking sheet and cut into 1/2 inch (12 mm) thick, 5 inch (12.5 cm) diameter disks. Bake for 30-45 minutes.

Marinated Portabello Mushrooms

1 oz.	Balsamic vinegar	25 ml
3 oz.	Olive oil	75 ml
1 sprig	Fresh thyme, leaves only	1 sprig
to taste	Salt and pepper	to taste
4	Portabello mushrooms	4

Whisk the oil, vinegar, thyme, salt and pepper together. Pour over the mushrooms. Grill each side for 1-2 minutes.

Double Cooked Angus Striploin

2 lbs.	Angus striploin	900 g
3 sprigs	Fresh thyme	3 sprigs
4 oz.	Bacon, cut into strips	125 g
6 oz.	Veal or beef stock	175 ml

| 4 | Cloves | 4 |
| 3 | Whole star anise | 3 |

Garnish

1/2 cup	Pecans	125 ml
3 tbsp.	Maple syrup	45 ml
to taste	Scallions, julienned	to taste

Preheat oven to 350°F (180°C). Sear all sides of the striploin in a frying pan on high to contain the juices. Cut the strip of fat off the side of the steak and put the thyme in its place. Secure by wrapping bacon strips around the steak, overlapping each piece. Bake in the oven for 30 minutes or until desired temperature has been reached. Cool and slice into 1/8inch (3 mm) shavings.

Heat half of the veal/beef jus, which should be a rich, thick stock that has been reduced to a silky consistency with the cloves. Let it simmer and reduce again by a quarter. Reheat the shaved beef in the liquid. Heat the remaining stock with the star anise, reducing by half to make the Star Anise Sauce. In a heated frying pan, toast pecans and toss with maple syrup just before serving.

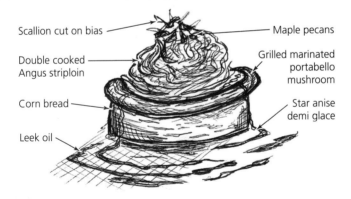

Scallion cut on bias — Maple pecans

Double cooked Angus striploin — Grilled marinated portabello mushroom

Corn bread — Star anise demi glace

Leek oil

Assembly: Place one round of corn bread in the centre of a plate with a grilled mushroom covering it. Top with a generous serving of double cooked beef. Drizzle the star anise sauce over the top. Garnish with maple pecans and julienned scallions. Serve immediately.

Dobrosav Kovacevic, Executive Chef
A Kettle of Fish

Flash Grilled Albacore Tuna
in Fragrant Filipino Lime and Dried Shitake Broth with Ponzu Marinated Soba Noodles

Serves: 4

4 x 4 oz.	Albacore tuna steaks	4 x 125 g

Dried Shitake Broth

6 cloves	Fresh garlic, minced	6 cloves
2	Large onions, minced	2
10 oz.	Fresh ginger root, minced	300 g
2 stalks	Lemongrass	2 stalks
10	Kaffir lime leaves	10
1 tbsp.	Canola oil	15 ml
3	Thai bird chileis	3
12 cups	Fish stock	2.75 litres
15	Shitake mushrooms, dried	15
8 oz.	"Kalamansi" Filipino lime juice, canned frozen concentrate	250 ml
to taste	Fish sauce, salt and pepper	to taste
14 oz.	Canned coconut milk	395 ml

Sweat garlic, onion, ginger, lemongrass and lime leaves in oil. After 2 minutes add Thai bird chilies and fish stock, shitake mushrooms and lime juice. Simmer for 1 hour. Strain and reserve shitake mushrooms and broth separately. Return strained broth to pot and simmer another 20 minutes. Check and season to taste with fish sauce, check again, season with salt and pepper.

Noodles

1 1/2 tbsp.	Konbu (dried seaweed)	25 ml
1 tbsp.	Bonito flakes (dried fish)	15 ml
8 oz.	Dried soba noodles	250 g
1/4 cup	Soya sauce	50 ml
2	Lemons, juiced	2
1/8 cup	Sesame oil	25 ml
1/8 cup	Peanut oil	25 ml

Boil 8 cups (2 litres) of water. When water comes to a boil, reduce heat to a very low simmer and add konbu. Simmer for about

10 minutes. Remove from heat and add bonito flakes. Cover and let stand for 30 minutes. Strain and using the strained liquid, boil noodles to *al dente*. Strain, toss with remaining ingredients and set aside to chill.

Daikon Root

1/2 cup	Sugar	125 ml
1 cup	Vinegar, white wine	250 ml
to taste	Salt and white pepper	to taste
1	Daikon radish, large	1
1/4 cup	Cilantro leaves	50 ml

Boil sugar and white wine vinegar, season with salt and white pepper. Reduce to a simmer for about 10 minutes. Using a vegetable peeler, peel ribbons of daikon. Pour the vinegar over the daikon and set aside.

Grill tuna steaks so they are still rare in the middle. The timing will depend on the thickness of the steaks. Using a serving fork, twist the noodles so they stand as a mound in the middle of a soup bowl. Twirl the daikon ribbons, and lay them flat on the bowl. Rest the tuna on the daikon root and pour broth over tuna. Garnish with cilantro leaves.

Fish substitutes: Escolar, Ahi Tuna.

Tina Fineza, Chef
Bin 942 Restaurant

Oven Roasted Fraser Valley Poussin
with Caramelized Winter Root Vegetables and Okanagan Dried Fruit Gnocchi

Serves: 4

Okanagan Dried Fruit Gnocchi

1/8 cup each	Dried blueberries, cherries, and apricots	25 g each
to taste	Salt and cracked black pepper	to taste
4	Russet potatoes, medium	4
1/2 cup	Flour	125 ml
1	Egg, beaten	1
1/2 cup	Parsley, flat leaf, chopped	125 ml

Chop all dried fruit and season with a dash of salt and cracked black pepper. Boil potatoes in their skins and when fully cooked, peel while the potatoes are still hot. Working very quickly, pass the potatoes through a ricer into a bowl. Add dried fruit and gently mix to incorporate. Add egg and gently add flour until mixture becomes workable. Cover bowl with a cloth to keep mixture warm.

Using a bit of flour, quickly dust a rolling surface and pinch off enough dough to form a long log. Cut into 1inch (2.5 cm) little logs and roll with the back of a fork. Do this to all the dough. Place individual logs onto wax paper and refrigerate. Boil salted water in a deep pot. Put small batches of gnocchi into the pot and when they float to the surface they are done. Set aside.

Amaretto Brown Butter Sauce

3 cups	Amaretto	750 ml
1/2 cup	Tamarind juice	125 ml

Reduce the two ingredients to form a syrup and set aside.

Poussin

Poussin is a young chicken, raised for eating.

2	Poussin, cut in half, second wing bone removed	2
1	Celery root, small, cut in wedges	1
1	Parsnip, medium, cut in circles	1
1	Yam, cut in half	1
1	Beet, medium, cut in wedges	1
2/3 cup	Butter	150 ml
1/2 cup	Slivered almonds	125 ml
	Oil for frying	

Pan sear the poussin in oil and add the vegetables. Finish in the oven at 350°F (180°C). Remove poussin and vegetables and add 4 tbsp. (60 ml) of butter. Butter will begin to foam and turn brown. Add amaretto syrup and whisk gently. Add another 1 tbsp. (15 ml) of butter and whisk gently. In another pan, melt 4 tbsp. (60 ml) of butter and do the same thing: when the butter foams and starts to turn brown, add the gnocchi. As soon as the gnocchi is hot all the way through add the almonds.

Assembly: Stack a few vegetables in the centre of the plate and surround them with gnocchi. Set poussin on top of vegetables and pour Amaretto Brown Butter Sauce around the vegetables. Garnish with slivered almonds.

Wine suggestion: Jammy Zinfandel

Tina Fineza, Chef
Bin 942 Restaurant

Macaroni and Cheese

Serves: 4

2 tsp.	Vegetable oil	10 ml
1/2 lb.	Bacon, Irish smoked or double-smoked, finely diced	250 g
4	Shallots, finely chopped	4
1/2 cup	Amsterdammer cheese, grated	125 ml
1/4 cup	Blue cheese	50 ml
1/2 cup	Parmigiano-Reggiano, grated	125 ml
8 cups	Cooked pasta, *al dente* (4 cups raw pasta)	1.8 kg

Béchamel Sauce

4 cups	Milk	1 litre
2 cloves	Fresh garlic, crushed	2 cloves
4 tbsp.	Unsalted butter	60 ml
4 tbsp.	All-purpose flour	60 ml
pinch	Nutmeg, freshly grated	pinch
to taste	Salt and white pepper	to taste

Combine milk with garlic in a saucepan on medium heat. Bring to a boil and remove from heat. Cover and leave to infuse for 10 minutes. Strain through a fine-mesh strainer. To make the roux, melt butter in a heavy saucepan on medium heat. Whisk in flour and cook for about 1 minute, until foaming. Remove from heat and allow it to cool slightly. Add strained hot milk, whisking constantly. Return saucepan to medium heat and bring mixture back to a boil, whisking constantly until the sauce thickens. Add nutmeg; season to taste with salt and freshly ground white pepper. Allow the sauce to simmer for a further 3 minutes.

Preheat the oven to 350°F (180°C). Heat vegetable oil in a frying pan on medium heat. Sauté bacon and shallots for about 5 minutes, until shallots are translucent and bacon is just cooked. Reheat béchamel and whisk in Amsterdammer, blue cheese and half of the Parmigiano-Reggiano. Add half of the bacon-shallot mixture. Divide cooked pasta into four, and put into individual casserole dishes. Pour sauce over them; enough to cover pasta by 1/2 inch (12 mm).

Sprinkle the tops with the remaining Parmigiano-Reggiano and bacon-shallot mixture. Bake in the oven for 10-15 minutes, until hot and bubbling. Place under a broiler until top is a light golden brown. Place casserole dish on a plate, lined with a napkin and serve immediately.

Robert Feenie, Executive Chef
Feenie's Vancouver

Potato wrapped Albacore Tuna Loin

Serves: 4

Curry Oil

Yields: 2 1/2 cups (725 ml)

1/4 cup	Carrot, diced	50 ml
1/4 cup	Onion, diced	50 ml
1/4 cup	Celery, diced	50 ml
1/3	Apple, diced	75 ml
2 tsp.	Red curry paste	10 g
1 1/2-2 cups	Grapeseed oil	375-500 ml
	or neutral flavoured vegetable oil	

Sweat vegetables with apples for 5 minutes — do not brown.
Add curry paste and cook for another 2-3 minutes. Add oil. Simmer
for 10 minutes and remove from heat. Let stand overnight to infuse
flavours. Strain leftover oil through cheesecloth.

Red Wine Sauce

Yields: 3 cups (750 ml)

1/2 cup	Red wine	125 ml
1/4 cup	Port	50 ml
2 tbsp.	Shallots, roughly chopped	30 ml
2 cloves	Garlic, crushed	2 cloves
2 sprigs	Thyme	2 sprigs
5	Black peppercorns, whole	5
4 1/3 cups	Strong veal stock	1 litre

Place shallots, peppercorns, garlic, port, wine and thyme in
saucepan and reduce to syrupy consistency. Add stock and reduce
by one third. Strain

Store the sauces in tightly sealed jars in the fridge. Curry oil is a
great addition to salad dressings or to toss on pasta... Be creative!

Potato wrapped Albacore Tuna Loin

3 cups	Peanut oil (for deep-frying)	750 ml
12 oz	British Columbia Albacore tuna, fresh	350 g
3 sheets	Dried nori seaweed,	3 sheets
3	Yukon Gold potatoes, large, peeled	3

Vegetables

1/2 cup	Chanterelle mushrooms	125 ml
1/2 cup	Fava beans, blanched	125 ml
1/2 cup	Green beans, blanched	125 ml
	Vegetable oil for sautéing	
to taste	Salt and pepper	to taste
1 tbsp. per serving	Curry oil	15 ml
1/3 cup per serving	Red wine reduction	75 ml

Place peanut oil in small saucepan, heat to 325°F (160°C). Pat tuna loin with paper towel to remove excess moisture. Season with salt and pepper. Dampen nori sheets with oil and water. Wrap loin with nori and put aside. With Japanese vegetable peeler, take the already peeled potatoes and make potato vermicelli or long thin peels of potato. Use only those peels that have not broken. Wrap the tuna loin without overlapping the potato, as it will not cook if layered. Pat potatoes dry, cut loin in half and carefully lower the tuna into the hot oil, covering completely. Cook until potato is golden brown and crispy; 4-5 minutes. Remove from oil and place on fresh sheet of paper towel to let excess oil drain. Lightly sauté vegetables in curry oil. Season to taste.

To serve: Spoon Red Wine Sauce onto a plate, top with sautéed chanterelles, beans and spinach. Butterfly tuna into 1 1/2-inch (3 cm) slices. Do not cut all the way through. Make about three cuts. Place on bed of vegetables and lightly drizzle curry oil around outside of plate.

Robert Feenie, Executive Chef
Lumière Restaurant

Ragout of Poached Chicken, Asparagus and Morels

Serves: 4

4 1/2 lb.	Chicken, free range	2 kg
to taste	Salt and pepper	to taste
1/2	Lemon, roughly chopped	1/2
to taste	Garlic cloves, smashed	to taste
to taste	Thyme, fresh sprigs	to taste

Wash chicken and pat dry. Season inside of cavity with salt and white pepper. Stuff the inside with lemon, garlic and thyme. Truss chicken. Refrigerate until ready to use.

Poaching Liquid

1/2	Leek, roughly chopped and washed	1/2
2	Carrots, peeled and roughly chopped	2
2	Celery stalks, washed and roughly chopped	2
1	Onion, peeled and roughly chopped	1
6 cloves	Garlic, peeled and smashed	6 cloves
8 sprigs	Thyme	8 sprigs
1	Bay leaf	1
10	Black peppercorns, crushed	10

In a large pot, add leeks, carrots, celery, onion, garlic, thyme, bay leaf, and peppercorns. Add enough water to cover chicken. Season water with salt. Bring to a boil. Add chicken. When water comes back up to a boil, turn the heat down to allow liquid to simmer. You should allow 15-20 minutes cooking time per pound of chicken.

When coooked, the chicken should easily fall away from the bone and the juices should be clear. When the chicken is cooked thoroughly, remove from liquid, cover with foil and allow it to rest. This allows the juices to redistribute throughout the chicken, ensuring a moister product.

Asparagus

1/2 lb.	Green asparagus	250 g
1/2 lb.	White asparagus	250 g

Bring two large pots of salted water to a boil. To clean green asparagus, snap or trim off fibrous ends. Peel the stalks or, if you prefer more colour, leave them as they are.To clean white asparagus, trim 1 inch (2.5 cm) from the bottom and discard. Peel asparagus from just below the tip, downward.

In one pot place green asparagus and cook for 2-3 minutes until tender but still firm and bright green. Immediately plunge or "shock" into ice water to stop cooking process and preserve colour. Remove asparagus and drain on paper towel. Place white asparagus in another pot and allow to simmer for 4 minutes. Turn off heat and allow it to sit for another 3 minutes. Remove and immediately shock in ice water. Remove asparagus and drain on paper towel.

Cut both white and green asparagus into two-inch pieces and refrigerate until ready to use.

Sauce

4 tbsp.	Unsalted butter	50 ml
1/2 lb.	Morels, trimmed and washed	250 g
to taste	Salt and white pepper	to taste
1/2 cup	Marsala	125 ml
1/2 cup	Heavy cream	125 ml

In a large skilled over medium-high heat, add 2 tbsp. (30 ml) unsalted butter. Add morels and sauté. Season with salt and ground white pepper. Continue to cook mushrooms until browned. Turn off the heat, add marsala and continue to cook over medium heat until liquid is reduced by half. Add cream and reduce by one-third. Whisk in remaining butter and re-adjust seasoning. Add asparagus pieces and chicken pieces to reheat.

To serve: Divide among four bowls and serve immediately.

Robert Feenie, Executive Chef
Lumière Restaurant

Crab Ravioli

Yields: 30 ravioli, 3 inches (8 cm) in diameter.

Pasta Dough

3 1/2 cups	Flour, all purpose	875 ml
1 cup	Semolina	250 ml
1 tsp.	Salt	5 ml
7	Eggs	7
2 tbsp.	Olive oil	30 ml

Combine the flour and semolina with the salt. Make a well in the centre and add the eggs and olive oil. Start to mix with a fork or by hand, slowly incorporating the flour as you go. Once the mixture is too stiff to mix by hand, use a dough scraper to finish combining. Knead by hand to form a uniform dough, then double wrap with cellophane and let rest at least 30 minutes prior to use.

Crab Filling

2 cups	Dungeness crab	500 ml
2 tbsp.	Leek brunoise, (finely diced) white and light green parts only	30 ml
1 tbsp.	Carrot brunoise	15 ml
1 tbsp.	Celery brunoise	15 ml
2 tbsp.	Chives, minced	30 ml
2 tbsp.	Clarified butter	30 ml
3 tbsp.	Mascarpone cheese	45 ml
to taste	Salt, pepper, lemon juice	to taste

Pick through the crab thoroughly and make sure there are no shell bits or cartilage. Sweat the vegetable brunoise gently in clarified butter until soft. When the vegetables are cool, combine all ingredients and mix well with a spoon. Season with salt, pepper and lemon juice.

Roll the dough as thinly as possible. Cut desired shapes — square or round (use a glass). Place a spoonful of filling in the middle of a piece of pasta and then lightly brush edges of pasta with water before sealing them. Cook ravioli in salted water for 2-3 minutes Before serving, drizzle with olive oil and parmesan cheese.

James Walt, Executive Chef
Blue Water Café and Raw Bar

Flaming Prawns

Serves: 4 as appetizer or 2 as a main course

1 tbsp.	Olive oil	15 ml
1 tsp.	Garlic, minced	5 ml
24	Prawns, large, peeled, de-veined	24
1/2 cup	Sweet red peppers, roasted and coarsely chopped	125 ml
1/2 cup	Plum tomatoes, canned, well drained and coarsely chopped	125 ml
1/2 cup	Feta cheese, crumbled	125 ml
1/4 cup	Fresh basil leaves	60 ml
1 oz.	Ouzo	30 ml
1/2	Lemon, seeds removed	1/2

In a large frying pan, heat olive oil over high heat. Add garlic, and when it sizzles, add the prawns and stir-fry until they turn pink. Add roasted peppers and tomatoes and continue stirring until the prawns are cooked through. While the prawns are cooking, heat a heavy, preferably cast-iron frying pan over high heat. Prepare a wooden board to place the frying pan on while you flame the prawns.

Add the feta and basil to the prawns, stir to combine. Transfer the prawns to one side of the hot frying pan and place the pan on the board. Carry the board to the table and advise everyone to stay well back. Pour the ouzo into the empty side of the pan and ignite immediately with a long match. Squeeze the lemon over the prawns to douse the flames, then give the prawns a stir. If pyrotechnics are not your style, just add the ouzo to the prawns after they have finished cooking. Serve with pasta, rice or bread to mop up the juices.

Karen Barnaby, Executive Chef
The Fish House in Stanley Park

Baccala Gratinato
con Pinoli e Sultanina
(Baked Salt Cod with Pine Nuts and Raisins)

Serves: 4

1 lb.	Salt cod	450 g
4/5 cup	Milk	200 ml
1/2 lb.	Onions, finely chopped	250 g
2 oz.	Butter	60 g
5 1/2 oz.	Cream	150 g
2 oz.	Reggiano cheese, grated	50 g
to taste	Pepper	to taste

Soak the fish overnight in cold water. The following day change the water and soak another 4 hours. Drain. Break up the fish into small pieces. Cook fish in milk for 10 minutes. Sweat onions in butter. Add cream and reduce for 15 minutes. Add fish and cheese. Cook over low heat until it takes on the consistency of mashed potatoes. Season with fresh ground pepper. Turn the mixture out into a baking dish and bake at 300°F (150°C) until golden brown, about 15–20 minutes.

Sauce

1/2 cup	Fish stock	100 ml
1/2 cup	Cream	100 ml
1 tbsp.	Raisins	15 ml
1 tbsp.	Pine nuts, toasted	15 ml

Bring fish stock to a boil. Add cream and simmer for 10 minutes. Add raisins and pine nuts and cook for 5 minutes. Season to taste.

Stéphan Meyer, Chef
Piccolo Mondo

Desserts &
Special Drinks

Pera in Port Syrup

Serves: 4

1 cup	Red wine	250 ml
1 cup	Water	250 ml
1 stick	Cinnamon	1 stick
2	Cloves	2
4 tbsp.	Sugar	60 ml
2 oz.	Walnuts	60 g
4	Pears, peeled and cored	4

Combine all ingredients except pears in a small pot and bring to a boil. Add pears, cook until soft and remove to let cool. Stuff with the walnuts and drizzle with Port Syrup.

Port Syrup

3 oz.	Sugar	90 g
6 oz.	Port	175 ml

Dissolve sugar in port while stirring. Stop stirring, bring to a boil and let cool.

Manuel Ferreira, Chef/Owner
Le Gavroche

Okanagan Apple Tart Tatin
with Maple Syrup Ice Cream

Serves: 6

Tart Tatin

3 1/2 oz.	Sugar	100 g
4	Okanangan apples, gala or golden	4
	delicious, peeled, cored and quartered	
1/2	Vanilla bean	1/2
2 oz.	Butter	50 g
1 1/2 tbsp.	Raisins, soaked in rum	20 g
6	Puff pastry disks	6
	Egg wash	

Make caramel by melting sugar over medium-high heat. Add apples and cook them in the caramel with the vanilla bean. Add butter and raisins. Fill the bottom of the 6 ramekins with apple mixture (this is an up side down type of tart) adding some caramel to cover. Place the 6 disks of puff pastry on top. Seal with egg wash and bake in a bain-marie at 375°F (190°C) for 35 minutes.

Maple Syrup Ice Cream

1 cup	Homogenized milk	250 ml
1 cup	Whipping cream, 36%	250 ml
4	Fresh farm egg, yolks	4
6 oz.	Maple syrup	170 ml

For the ice cream, warm the milk and cream together. Don't let it boil. Mix the egg yolks with the maple syrup. Slowly add the warm milk and cream to the egg mixture to temper it. Pour the mixture in a double boiler and stir constantly until it begins to thicken. Place into an ice cream maker to turn it into ice cream.

For assembly, turn tart upside down onto the serving plate, dust with icing sugar and top with the maple syrup ice cream. This will melt from the heat of the tart and form a complimentary sauce, creating a pleasant hot–warm contrast.

Pino Posteraro, Executive Chef/Owner
Cioppino's

Amaretti

Serves: 24

1 cup	Almonds, blanched and sliced	250 ml
1/2 tbsp	Cornstarch	7 ml
1/2 cup	Icing sugar	125 ml
2	Egg whites	2
6 tbsp.	White sugar	90 ml
1/4 tsp	Almond extract	1 ml

Preheat oven to 300°F (150°C).

Combine the sliced almonds and cornstarch in a food processor. Blend until finely ground. Add icing sugar and pulse until combined.

Whip egg whites and white sugar until stiff peaks form. Gently fold the almond mixture and extract into the stiff whites. Place mixture in a piping bag with a small round tip. Pipe "toonie sized" (30 mm) rounds onto a greased or silicone paper lined baking sheet, leaving 1/4 inch (6 mm) between each round. Bake for 35-40 minutes. Remove and allow to cool before serving.

Dino Gazzola, Executive Chef
Bridges Restaurant

Sweet Plantain
with Guava and fruit

Serves: 4

1/2	Ripe plantain	1/2
3 tbsp.	Shredded mozzarella	45 ml
3 tbsp.	Guava paste	45 ml
1/2 cup	Orange juice	125 ml
1	Apple	1
5	Strawberries	5
1	Mango	1
2 tbsp.	Plain yogurt	30 ml
2 cups	Canola oil	500 ml

Preheat the oven at 350°F (180°C).

Heat the oil in a deep pot. Cut the plantain into four pieces crosswise and deep fry them until slightly brown; remove and dry excess oil. Place a round mould in the middle of an oven proof, medium-sized plate. Press two pieces of plantain into the mould with the back of a spoon. Add half the cheese and top with the remaining plantain, followed by the remaining cheese. Put the plate in the oven until the cheese melts; for about 3 minutes. Meanwhile, in a hot pan, heat the guava paste and orange juice until smooth. Set aside and keep warm. Make a fruit salad with the apple, strawberries and mango. When the cheese is melted take the plate out of the oven and drizzle some of the guava-orange syrup over the top. Top with fruit salad and yogurt. Serve while it is warm.

Serving suggestions: This dish can be served as a dessert or as a brunch item. It goes well with coffee or tropical juice.

Pablo Rojas, Chef/Owner
Baru Latino Restaurant

Buttermilk Pie

Yields: 10 inch (25 cm) pie (12 servings)

Crust

1/2 cup	Almonds, toasted, finely chopped	125 ml
1/2 cup	Hazelnuts, toasted, finely chopped	125 ml
1 cup	Graham wafer crumbs	250 ml
1/2 cup	Butter, melted and slightly browned	125 ml
1 tsp.	Coriander seeds, toasted and ground	5 ml
1/2 tsp.	Fennel seeds, toasted and ground	2 ml

Mix well and press into 10 inch (25 cm) pie pan.

Filling

1 lb.	Cream cheese, room temperature	450 g
2/3 cup	Sugar	150 ml
3	Eggs	3
1 tsp.	Vanilla	5 ml
3/4 cup	Buttermilk	175 ml
1 1/3 cups	Coronation grapes	325 ml

Preheat oven the to 300°F (150°C). Beat cream cheese and sugar together until smooth. Beat the eggs and vanilla together. Slowly add the eggs to the cream cheese mixture, scraping down the sides of the bowl until smooth. Slowly add the buttermilk, beating to combine. Distribute the grapes evenly over the pie crust. Pour the batter into the crust and bake for 30-40 minutes. The pie should still be slightly jiggly in the middle. Cool to room temperature and refrigerate for at least 6 hours before cutting.

Substitutes: Blueberries, raspberries or cranberries may be used in place of the grapes.

Karen Barnaby, Executive Chef
The Fish House in Stanley Park

Golden Pineapple Carpaccio
with Coriander and Lime Sorbet

Serves: 8

This signature dessert from Thomas Haas is the perfect ending to a summer dinner party. Simple, refreshing and tangy, the intense pineapple and citrus flavours will dance on your plate.

40	Coriander leaves	40
8 oz.	Granulated sugar	240 g
4	Vanilla beans, whole	4
1	Hawaiian pineapple	1
1 oz.	Icing sugar	30 g
	Coriander and lime sorbet	

Blend coriander leaves and granulated sugar until thoroughly mixed and dark green in colour. Slice the vanilla beans in half lengthwise and remove the seeds. Blend vanilla seeds with the coriander-sugar mixture.

Place 8 round pineapple slices on a silicon or wax paper-lined baking sheet in the oven and dry at 280°F (140°C) for about 35 minutes until the slices are golden and crispy. When cool, place the dried pineapple in an airtight container until needed.

Arrange uncooked pineapple pieces, sliced paper thin, on eight dessert plates. Sprinkle fruit with the coriander sugar. Garnish with a quenelle (scoop) of sorbet. Place one baked pineapple slice in the sorbet.

Wine suggestion: Black Hills "Sequentia", Okanagan Valley, 2000.

Thomas Haas, Executive Pastry Chef
Diva at the Met

Portuguese Flan
with Port and Vanilla

Serves: 16

This recipe marries the best of a crème brûlée and a crème caramel.
It is rich and smooth, enhancing the bold flavour of any good port.

2 cups	Sugar, white granulated	500 ml
1 cup	Warm water	250 ml
4 cups	Whipping cream	1 litre
2 strips	Orange rind	2 strips
1/4 cup	Port wine	50 ml
1	Vanilla bean	1
13	Egg yolks, large	13
16	Ovenproof ceramic ramekins	16
	Butter for ramekins	

In a heavy-bottomed pot place 1 cup (250 ml) of sugar in the
centre. Add warm water by pouring it around the sugar. Bring this
mixture to a boil and simmer until the sugar begins to caramelize.
To avoid crystallization, make sure not to stir or shake the pot .
Using a pastry brush, clean the sides of the pot with warm water to
dissolve any crystals that may form. When the sugar is a deep amber
colour, remove the pot from the heat and carefully swirl in about
3 spoonfuls of hot water. This will stop the sugar from continuing to
cook. Pour this caramelized sugar into the 16 buttered ramekins
about 1/4 inch (5 mm) deep. Set aside.

Bring the cream, the remaining sugar, orange rind, port and seeds
from the vanilla bean to a boil, then remove from heat. Put all the
egg yolks into another bowl and slowly "temper" them by pouring
half of the heated cream mixture slowly into the yolks, whisking
constantly. Then whisk the egg and cream mixture back into the
remaining hot cream. Strain mixture through a fine sieve and then
fill the ramekins. Bake uncovered in a 2 inch (5 cm) deep baking pan
half filled with water, for about 45 minutes, at 325°F (160°C).
Remove from oven and cool in the fridge for at least 8 hours. To
serve, flip upside down on a plate and gently shake. They should
slide out with ease.

Sylvain Cuerrier, Executive Chef
The Observatory Restaurant at Grouse Mountain

Warm Belgium Chocolate Cake

Serves: 8

1 cup	Butter, soft, unsalted	250 g
1 cup	Dark chocolate, semi-sweet	250 g
	Valrhona or other quality brand	
1 oz.	Espresso or strong dark coffee	30 g
4 oz.	Flour	125 g
4 oz.	Granulated sugar	125 g
pinch	Salt	pinch
4	Eggs	4
4	Egg yolks	4
	Butter and sugar to coat ramekins	

Preheat oven to 400°F (200°C).

Combine the butter and chocolate in a bowl over a bain-marie (water bath). Add the shot of espresso. Heat gently until the chocolate and butter is just melted. Stir frequently with a spatula. Allow the mixture to cool to lukewarm. Add the flour, sugar and salt and whisk until well combined. Add the eggs and egg yolks. Whisk until completely mixed. Allow batter to rest for 5 minutes, then mix again with a wooden spoon or spatula. Prepare 8 individual ramekins by coating with a thin layer of butter followed by a thin coating of sugar. Spoon batter into the ramekins, filling three quarters to the top. Bake for approximately 10 minutes. The cake will be firm on the outside but warm and liquid in the middle.

Serving suggestion: Serve with vanilla or hazelnut ice cream.

James Walt, Executive Chef
Blue Water Café and Raw Bar

Torta Milano

Serves: 8-10

Amaretti Crust

2/3 cup	Almonds, blanched	150 ml
1/2 cup	Icing sugar	125 ml
1/3 cup	Cornstarch	75 ml
1/4 cup	Egg whites	50 ml
1/3 cup	Sugar	75 ml
1 tsp.	Almond extract	5 ml
	Butter, cold	

In a food processor, grind almonds, icing sugar and cornstarch. Beat the egg whites with sugar until it forms soft peaks, and then add almond extract. Fold in the almond mixture.

Preheat the oven to 400°F (200°C). Pipe or spoon into small mounds onto a lined baking pan and bake until dry; approximately 30 minutes. When cooled, pulverize in a food processor with the cold butter just so that it binds. Spread mixture across the bottom of a 12 inch (30 cm) spring-form pan and bake 350°F (180°C) degrees until golden brown, approximately 10 minutes.

Mascarpone Mousse

3	Egg yolks	3
1/4 cup	Sugar	50 ml
1/2 cup	Mascarpone cheese	125 ml
2	Gelatin packages	2
1 tbsp.	Lemon juice	15 ml
1 tsp.	Almond extract	5 ml
1 cup	Whipping cream	250 ml

Beat the yolks with sugar and fold in mascarpone. Dissolve the gelatin in warm lemon juice and add the almond extract. Fold in the mascarpone mixture. Whip the cream to a ribbon consistency and fold into the mascarpone mixture; set aside in the fridge.

Dark Chocolate Mousse

| 1 cup | Dark chocolate* | 250 ml |
| 2 cups | Whipped cream | 500 ml |

Melt the chocolate, fold in the whipped cream, and pour into the bottom of the crust. Place the marscapone mixture into a piping bag and pipe out small rounds of the mixture over the dark mousse

Milk Chocolate Mousse

| 1 cup | Milk chocolate* | 250 ml |
| 2 cups | Whipped cream | 500 ml |

Melt the chocolate and fold in the whipped cream. Fill the remainder of the pan and refrigerate or freeze the torte.

Chocolate Glaze

| 2 cups | Chocolate* | 500 ml |
| 1 cup | Whipping cream, hot | 250 ml |

Add the chocolate to the warm cream and stir until melted. Remove the torte from the fridge and remove the outer pan. Glaze.

Refrigerate until serving. Enjoy!

This was our award winning dessert, which gave us the "Award of Excellence" back in 1998.

*We are so used to using the excellent quality of Callebaut chocolate that it is very hard to change our habits.

Lynda Larouche
The Teahouse Restaurant in Stanley Park at Ferguson Point

Date Halva

Serves: 10

7 oz.	Pitted dates	200 g
1 tsp.	Butter, unsalted	5 ml
1 tbsp.	Almonds	15 ml
1 tbsp.	Pistachio nuts, shelled	15 ml
1 tsp.	Unsweetened coconut, fine	5 ml

Warm dates in small pan over very low heat until softened. Stir once or twice to ensure even heating. Meanwhile cut almonds into 8 pieces. Cut pistachios in half. Purée warmed dates in food processor until supple, like dough. Brush 1 sheet of wax paper (10 inches or 25 cm square) with butter. Spread dates on the paper and flatten. Place another sheet (same size as the first) on top of the dates and using a rolling pin, press dates to spread evenly. Lift top sheet and evenly spread almonds and pistachios over the top. Cover with top sheet and roll again. Remove date mixture from paper and roll dates into a tube. Roll tube in coconut and wrap with waxed paper. Cut in half lengthwise and put in fridge to set.

This recipe yields two, 5 inch (12.5 cm) rolls, 1 inch (2.5 cm) in diameter. When cold, slice into wheels 1/4 inch (5 mm) thick to serve.

Krishna Jamal, Executive Chef
Rubina Tandoori

Caramelized Pear Tarts

Yields: 6 tarts, each 4 inch (10 cm) in diameter.

Pastry

3/4 cup	Flour	175 ml
1/4 cup	Cornmeal	60 ml
2 tsp.	Sugar	10 ml
1/2 tsp.	Salt	2.5 ml
1/4 cup	Butter	60 ml
2 tbsp.	Cold water	30 ml

Preheat the oven to 400°F (200°C). Combine flour, cornmeal, sugar and salt in a bowl. Cut butter into small pieces and work into flour mixture until the texture becomes mealy. Add water and stir until just combined. Cover and allow mixture to rest for 20 minutes. Divide dough into 6 pieces and roll out on a lightly floured surface to form rounds 4 inches (10 cm) in diameter.

Filling

1/2 cup	Sugar	125 ml
1/4 cup	Butter	60 ml
3	Pears, Bartlett **or** Anjou	3

Make caramel by combining sugar and butter in a saucepan on medium heat; cook until golden, 3-4 minutes. Pour 2 tbsp. (30 ml) of caramel into each tart pan. Peel, core and halve pears. Place a half pear, cored side down, on top of the caramel in each pan. Place a pastry round on top of each half pear, pressing down around it to follow the shape of the fruit. Bake in the oven until pastry is golden and pear is cooked through, about 20 minutes. Remove from the oven and allow it to rest for 5 minutes.

To serve: Invert tarts onto individual warmed plates.

Dennis Green, Executive Chef
Bishop's

Apple Banana Spring Roll
with Coconut Ice Cream

Serves: 4

1	Apple, peeled, cubed	1
3 tbsp.	Sake	45 ml
1 1/2 tbsp.	Sugar	23 ml
pinch	Salt	pinch
1	Banana, julienned	1
4	Spring roll wrappers	4
1	Egg white, lightly beaten	1
	Oil for deep frying	
garnish	Orange segments	garnish
	and puréed strawberries	
	Coconut ice cream	

Cook apple with sake in a saucepan over low heat until tender. Add sugar and salt. Mash the apple and continue to cook until a paste is formed. Set aside to cool. Place a spring roll wrapper on a board in a diamond orientation. Place two or three pieces of banana just below the centre of the wrapper. Spread 2 tsp. (10 ml) of the apple paste along the length of the banana pieces. Brush egg white on the corners of the wrapper. Fold the bottom corner up and over the banana and apple. Fold the two side corners in and continue to roll to form a neat parcel, ensuring the edges are well sealed with the egg white. Heat the oil to 300°F (150°C). Fry the rolls for 1 1/2 minutes until golden brown.

To serve: Place a single scoop of coconut ice cream at the centre of each of four plates. Cut fried spring rolls into two on a diagonal and arrange on each side of the ice cream. Drizzle a small amount of sauce over the ice cream and place a segment of orange on top.

Hidekazu Tojo, Executive Chef/Owner
Tojo's

Gulab Jaman
(Milk Balls in Syrup)

Serves: 6

2 cups	Sugar	500 g
2 tbsp.	Water	30 ml

Combine sugar and water in a saucepan, bring to a strong boil and remove from heat. Set aside to cool.

5 oz.	Milk powder	140 g
2 oz.	Flour, all purpose	55 g.
1/4 lb.	Butter, melted	125 g
1/4 tsp.	Baking powder	1 ml
8 cups	Canola oil	2 litres

Mix milk powder, flour, baking powder and butter. Add a touch of water and knead into smooth dough. Set aside and let the dough rise. Divide into small round balls the size of walnuts. When oil is heated, fry the balls until they are a light golden brown. Remove from oil and place balls in syrup. Marinate for a minimum of 2-3 hours. Serve either warm or cold.

Kan Singh, Chef/Owner
Akbar's Own Dining Lounge

Chocolate and Passion Fruit Truffle Torte

Yields: 8 inch (20 cm) spring form pan

Genoise

2	Eggs	2
1/3 cup	Sugar	75 ml
pinch	Salt	pinch
10 oz.	Butter, melted	285 g
1 tbsp.	Cocoa	15 ml
3/8 cup	Flour	85 ml

Preheat the oven to 350°F (180°C). With electric mixer, beat eggs with sugar and salt until approximately tripled in volume. Gently fold in melted butter, sift cocoa and flour into mixture and try not to deflate the mixture. Pour into a spring form pan lined with parchment and bake for approximately 15 minutes, or until an inserted skewer comes out clean. Cool for 5 minutes, remove form and finish cooling completely on a wire rack.

Syrup

1/2 cup	Water	125 ml
4 oz.	Sugar	125 g
1/2	Orange, juice	1/2

Put all ingredients into a pot, bring to a boil then remove from heat and set aside.

Ganache

11 1/2 oz.	Bittersweet chocolate, good quality	325 g
2/3 cup	Heavy cream	150 ml
2/3 cup	Passion fruit purée	150 ml
6 tbsp.	Unsalted butter, room temperature cut into 12 pieces	90 ml

Melt chocolate over double boiler and set aside. Separately scald cream and purée, pour over chocolate and whisk to combine. Add butter pieces and gently mix until completely melted.

Assembly: Trim Genoise to a level disc of approximately 1/3 inch (8 mm) high and return to spring form. Brush syrup over Genoise to moisten, then pour Ganache over cake and refrigerate for a minimum of 4 hours.

Note: The Genoise can be made a day ahead and wrapped tightly, stored in the refrigerator. The torte can be allowed to set overnight. Left over Genoise can be used to make rum balls.

Jonathan Thauberger, Executive Chef
Delilah's

Coffee Toffee Pots de Crème

Serves: 12

3 cups	Sugar	750 ml
3/4 cup	Water	175 ml
3 cups	Milk	750 ml
3 cups	Cream	750 ml
6 oz.	Kahlua liquor	175 ml
18	Egg yolks	18

In a large, heavy-bottomed saucepan, dissolve sugar and water together to create a caramel. While caramel is cooking, slowly bring milk and cream to a simmer. As soon as the caramel turns golden amber, remove from heat and slowly pour the milk mixture into it. It is best to do this over a sink because it can bubble over. Whisk this mixture into the egg yolks and strain. Skim all the air bubbles off and cool in a water bath. When it has thoroughly cooled, refrigerate for at least one hour.

Preheat the oven to 325°F (160°C). Pour mixture into 6 oz. (170 g) ramekins and cook covered with foil in a bain-marie for about 55 minutes. To check, only a spot in the middle the size of a nickel should be jiggly and the sides should be set. Take out and cool on racks. Wrap individually with plastic wrap and refrigerate for 4-6 hours or overnight.

Wine suggestions: Serve with a sparkling dessert wine such as Moscato D'Asti or a German style Riesling.

Tina Fineza, Chef
Bin 942 Restaurant

Fennel Vanilla Ice Cream

Serves: 4-6

2	Fennel bulbs, trimmed	2
1	Large vanilla bean, pulp of	1
1 cup	Heavy cream	250 ml
1 cup	Whole milk	250 ml
5	Egg yolks, large	5
1/2 cup	Sugar	125 ml

Using a mandoline, slice fennel bulbs paper-thin. Add sliced fennel and vanilla pulp to cream and milk. Combine cream, milk, fennel and vanilla pulp in a heavy saucepan. Bring liquid just to the boiling point over medium-high heat. In a stainless steel bowl, whisk yolks and sugar to a thick ribbon stage. Temper the yolk mixture by stirring in some of the hot cream/milk mixture. Slowly add the remaining hot cream mixture. Place mixture in a double boiler over simmering water and stir constantly until it reaches 175°F (80°C). Remove from heat. Strain and cool. Refrigerate overnight. Freeze in ice cream machine according to manufacturer's directions.

Robert Feenie, Executive Chef
Feenie's Vancouver

Apple Galette

Serves: 4-6, depending on thinness of puff pastry.

This galette is one of the initial desserts on the menu. It has been on since the beginning and continues to appear. It is a favourite of the chef's mother — a classic combination of puff pastry, frangipane, caramel and apples.

Frangipane

6 tbsp.	Unsalted butter	80 ml
1/4 cup	Icing sugar	50 ml
3/4 cup	Almonds, blanched, ground	175 ml
2 tbsp.	Flour, all purpose	30 ml
1	Whole egg, lightly beaten	1

Beat butter and icing sugar together until smooth. Add ground almonds and flour; mix well. Slowly add egg and mix until well incorporated. Refrigerate until ready to use.

Galette

2	Granny Smith apples, peeled and cored	2
1	Sheet puff pastry, thawed	1
2 tbsp.	Unsalted butter, melted	30 ml
2 tsp.	Granulated sugar	10 ml
1 tsp.	Ground cinnamon	5 ml

Preheat oven to 400°F (200°C). Cut puff pastry with a large round cookie cutter, 4-5 inches (10-12.5 cm) across. Use a smaller round cutter to imprint a guideline for the apples, leaving a 1/2 inch (12 mm) border. Slice apples thinly, about 1/8 inch (3 mm) thick. Place 1 tbsp. (15 ml) frangipane in the middle of puff pastry round and press gently to even out the top. Carefully place apple slices around in a fan pattern. Drizzle melted butter over apples; be careful not to let butter run over sides of puff pastry. Sprinkle with a mixture of the sugar and cinnamon. Place on parchment-lined baking sheet; bake for 10-15 minutes or until puff pastry is golden brown on bottom and apples are cooked.

Caramel Sauce

1 1/4 cups	Granulated sugar	300 ml
2 tbsp.	Water	30 ml
2 cups	Heavy cream	500 ml
2 tbsp.	Unsalted butter	30 ml

In a heavy-bottomed pot, boil the sugar with the water until it turns dark brown. Carefully stir in the cream (it might bubble up). Remove from heat. Stir in the butter.

To serve: Galettes can be served right away or cooled and reheated for a few minutes in medium oven before serving. Place apple galette in centre of plate. Dust with confectioners' sugar and place a scoop of ice cream (see page 125) on top. Drizzle caramel sauce around the galette. Serve immediately.

Robert Feenie, Executive Chef
Feenie's Vancouver

Okanagan Apple Cake

Serves: 12

2 cups	Flour, whole wheat	500 g
1/4 cup	Wheatgerm, toasted	50 ml
2 tsp.	Baking soda	10 ml
1 tsp.	Cinnamon	5 ml
1 tsp.	Salt	5 ml
1/2 tsp.	Nutmeg	2 ml
4	Tart apples, peeled and cored	4
1 cup	Sugar	250 ml
1 cup	Brown sugar	250 ml
1/2 cup	Vegetable oil	125 ml
1 cup	Walnuts, chopped	250 ml
2	Eggs, well beaten	2
1 tsp.	Vanilla	5 ml

Stir together flour, wheatgerm, soda, cinnamon, salt and nutmeg.
Set aside. In a large bowl, combine apples, sugars, oil, walnuts, eggs
and vanilla. Preheat oven to 350°F (180°C). Add flour mixture to
apple mixture, stirring gently with a wooden spoon. Blend well.
Turn into a greased 13 x 9 inch (33 x 23 cm) baking pan. Bake for
50 minutes or until the cake pulls away from the sides of the pan.
Cool on a rack. Sprinkle with confectioner's sugar. Slice into
12 bars.

Mark Jorundson, Chef
Rocky Mountaineer Railtours

Masala Chai
(Indian Spiced Tea)

Serves: 4

5 cups	Water	1.25 litres
1/4 tsp.	Spice mix (see below)	1 ml
2	2-cup tea bags (black tea)	2
1 cup	Milk	250 ml
4-8 tsp.	Sugar, to taste	20-40 ml

Boil water with spice mix. Reduce to 4 cups (1 litre). Add tea bags and boil for a minute. Add milk and boil for 2 minutes. Remove tea bags. Add sugar and serve hot.

Spice Mix

1 tbsp.	Ground ginger	15 ml
1 tbsp.	Ground black pepper	15 ml
2 tsp.	Garam Masala	10 ml

Use a coarse grind for spices and strain through a tea strainer so you don't get powder in your tea.

Garam Masala

4 tbsp.	Cinnamon	60 ml
1 tbsp.	Cloves	15 ml
1 tbsp.	Cardamom	15 ml
1 tsp.	Mace	5 ml

Toasting spices releases their flavours and adds an extra taste element. Use a heavy skillet, preferably without a non-stick surface. Heat the pan over low heat, add all the spices whole, toss and stir for about 2-4 minutes, as they cook. The minute you smell the toasty fragrance, remove them from the pan. Cool and grind. Blend together well.

Krishna Jamal, Executive Chef
Rubina Tandoori

Sweet or Fruit Lassi
(Yogurt Drinks)

Serves: 4

Lassi is a yogurt shake. You'll find it all over India in different forms.
In Punjab people drink sweet lassi and fruit flavoured lassi. In
Gujarat and southern India it's savoury, with salt, cumin and mint.
You may add black pepper for a tangy taste.

For each recipe blend the ingredients in a blender. For the fruit lassi,
mangos, raspberries, strawberries or blueberries are suitable.

Sweet Lassi

1 1/2 cups	Plain yogurt	375 ml
8 tsp.	Sugar	40 ml
2 cups	Ice cubes	500 ml

Fruit Lassi

1 1/2 cups	Plain yogurt	375 ml
2 tbsp.	Sugar	30 ml
1/2 cup	Crushed fruit	125 ml
1 1/2 cups	Ice cubes	375 ml

Krishna Jamal, Executive Chef
Rubina Tandoori

Martinis
Ranging from serious to flirtatious!

Milano

2 oz.	Gin	60 ml
1/8 oz.	Campari	4 ml
1/8 oz.	Cinzano	4 ml

Into an ice-filled martini shaker pour the gin, the Campari and Cinzano and shake or swirl. Strain into a chilled martini glass garnished with a lemon wedge.

Note: The amount of Campari and Cinzano can vary according to taste.

Devine

2 oz.	Vodka or Gin	60 ml
1/2 oz.	Dry white vermouth	15 ml
1 oz.	White grape juice	30 ml

Pour the gin or vodka into an ice-filled martini shaker, add the vermouth and grape juice, shake or swirl. Strain into a chilled martini glass garnished with frozen grapes (skewer the grapes before freezing).

Champs D'Alize

2 oz.	Vodka	60 ml
1 oz.	Alize Gold	30 ml
1 oz.	Passion fruit juice	30 ml
1 oz.	Champagne	30 ml

Into an ice-filled martini shaker pour the vodka, Alize Gold liqueur, passion fruit juice and top with champagne. Swirl and strain into a chilled martini glass garnished with a slice of tropical fruit — starfruit in season is amazing, or a kiwi slice or a honeydew melon ball.

Clarence Donkersgoed, Bar Manager
Delilah's

Triple Chocolate Martini

Serves: 4

Thomas Haas created this dessert for those with a passion for chocolate — luscious layers of velvety dark, white and milk chocolate are the perfect complement to a romantic dinner for two.

Dark Chocolate Cream

2 oz.	Chocolate, good quality bitter-sweet, chopped fine	55 g
6 tbsp.	Whipping cream	90 ml
2 1/2 tbsp.	Milk (2%), lukewarm	35 ml

Place chocolate in heatproof bowl set over saucepan of hot, not simmering, water until partially melted (the water should not touch the bottom of the bowl), stirring occasionally. Remove bowl from saucepan and continue stirring until melted and smooth.

Meanwhile, place whipping cream in a medium bowl and beat just until soft peaks form, set aside. Add lukewarm milk, all at once, to melted chocolate and stir with spatula (not a whisk). Add whipping cream, all at once, and stir with spatula until blended (mixture will be runny). Pour an equal portion of chocolate mixture into each of four 8 oz. (250 ml) martini glasses. Place in refrigerator for about 30-40 minutes or until set.

White Chocolate Cream

4 oz.	White chocolate, good quality, chopped fine	125 g
6 tbsp.	Whipping cream	90 ml
2 1/2 tbsp.	Milk (2%), lukewarm	35 ml

Start preparing white chocolate cream as soon as dark chocolate cream is set and prepare following the same directions as dark chocolate cream. Spoon an equal portion of white chocolate cream over dark chocolate cream in each martini glass. Place in refrigerator for about 1 1/2 hours or until set (takes longer to set than dark chocolate).

Note: To make ahead, once chocolate has set, glasses can be covered tightly with plastic wrap and refrigerated overnight. Next day add milk chocolate layer.

Milk Chocolate Cream

6 1/2 oz.	Milk chocolate, good quality, chopped fine	185 g
1/2 cup + 2 1/2 tbsp.	Whipping cream	125 ml + 35 ml
6 tbsp.	Milk (2%), lukewarm	90 ml

Start preparing milk chocolate cream as soon as white chocolate cream is set and prepare following the same directions as dark chocolate cream. Spoon an equal portion of milk chocolate cream over white chocolate cream in each martini glass. Place in refrigerator for about 1 1/2 hours or until set.

Note: To make ahead, once chocolate has set, glasses can be covered tightly with plastic wrap and refrigerated overnight.

Grand Marnier Sauce (optional)

4	Large egg yolks, whisked	4
1/4 cup	Granulated sugar	50 ml
3/4 cup	Whipping cream	175 ml
2 tsp.	Grand Marnier	10 ml

In medium heatproof bowl, whisk egg yolks and sugar together. Whisk in whipping cream. Place over simmering water and cook, stirring constantly, until mixture thickens slightly and coats a metal spoon. Pour through sieve set over bowl. Stir in Grand Marnier; let cool. Cover bowl with plastic wrap and refrigerate until ready to use.

Note: Sauce can be prepared up to one day ahead.

Thomas Haas, Executive Pastry Chef
Diva at the Met

Restaurants

Bacchus Restaurant and Piano Lounge

Walk through the Hornby Street entrance and Bacchus' attention to detail is immediately apparent. You are instantly surrounded by luxury; richly upholstered furniture, warm, dark wood and light fixtures personally imported from Venice by owner Eleni Skalbania. Frank Dodd is the European Chef who presides over the food of this Four Diamond establishment. Bacchus takes oenophiles on a tour of the world's finest vineyards, from the West Coast to France, Italy, South Africa and Australia.

Mon-Fri 6:30am-10pm, Sat-Sun 7am-10pm, Lounge open until 1am
• 604-608-5319 • 845 Hornby Street • www.wedgewoodhotel.com

Gusto di Quattro

Translated "Gusto di Quattro" means a taste of Quattro. Located by the Lonsdale Quay market, and a North Shore favourite since it opened its doors in September 2000, the restaurant has a long history. Chef Robert Parrott thoughtfully prepares the menu at Gusto di Quattro. He prides himself on the homemade pastas that made the Corsi family famous at this location so many years ago. Evenings at Gusto are lit by candlelight and appetites are whet by delectable antipasto platters followed by Quattro's famous pastas and main courses. Roasted Duck Breast with Frangelico, Toasted Pine Nuts and Grilled Orange is a recent addition.

Mon-Fri open for lunch from noon, dinner daily from 5pm
• 604-924-4444 • 1 Lonsdale Avenue, North Vancouver
• www.quattrorestaurants.com

Cioppino's Mediterranean Grill & Enoteca

Located in the Heart of Vancouver's trendy Yaletown, Cioppino's Mediterranean Grill offers a warm and elegant atmosphere with clean lines and an open kitchen. Enoteca is the more casual and rustic option to Cioppino's, although you can order from both menus. Restaurateur/owner Giuseppe Posteraro, known to his many friends as Pino, provides a fresh perspective on Mediterranean cooking. He'll surprise and refresh your taste buds with "Cucina Naturale" which is his forte. Both lunch and dinner menus reflect the seasonal availability of fish, game, fruits and vegetables. Since opening, Cioppino's has won the *Wine Spectator's* "Award of Excellence", Dirona's "Award of Excellence", and *Vancouver Magazine* Restaurant Awards "Best Italian/Mediterranean".

Mediterranean Grill
604-688-7466 • 1133 Hamilton Street • www.cioppinosyaletown.com
Enoteca
604-688-8462 • 1129 Hamilton Street

Prospect Point Restaurant

Prospect Point is located at the highest point in Stanley Park, overlooking the North Shore mountains, the Burrard Inlet and the Lions Gate Bridge. The Prospect Point lookout has been a landmark destination and a Vancouver tradition since the mid 1800s. Amenities include a café and renowned casual dining restaurant, famous for their salmon and West Coast cuisine. Choose to dine indoors or on the attractive patio.

Summer, daily 11am-11pm, Winter Mon-Thur 11:30am-4pm,

Fri-Sat 11:30am-8pm,
Sunday 11:00am-6pm
- 604-669-2737
- www.prospectpoint.ca

Diva at the Met

Located downtown in Vancouver's intimate Metropolitan Hotel, the highly acclaimed Diva at the Met performs under the direction of executive chef Scott Baechler. He and his culinary team to present "Contemporary Canadian" cuisine. Fresh, clean tastes dance together for an unforgettable dining experience in a modern and tiered room. Baechler's passion for cooking has earned Diva a reputation as one of Vancouver's best dining destinations. Pastry chef Thomas Haas, who creates award-winning classic desserts and signature chocolates that feature the season's best. Awarded "Best Last Course" by *Vancouver Magazine* Restaurant Critics for the last three consecutive years, the dessert and cheese menus at Diva at the Met are unrivaled in the city.

604-602-7788 • 645 Howe Street
- www.metropolitan.com

Bridges Restaurant

This elegant restaurant is located on the water's edge of Granville Island, a popular destination for both locals and visitors. With one of the most picturesque views in the city, few places offer better sunsets, with English Bay and Stanley Park in the background. Under the direction of Dino Gazzola, Bridges is known for featuring fresh seafood, lamb, beef, delectable desserts as well as a fully stocked bar and wine cellar. Sunday brunch is a special treat.

Dining room daily 5:30-midnight, Bistro daily 11am-midnight, Bar daily 11am-1am • 604-687-4400
- 1696 Duranleau
- www.bridgesrestaurant.com

Kirin Mandarin Restaurant

The Kirin Restaurant Group has a reputation among food connoisseurs both locally and overseas for providing its customers with a memorable dinning experience. Over the years their efforts have been well recognized with numerous awards. They serve only the finest quality food meticulously prepared, complemented by unsurpassed service in a comfortable ambience. Kirin specializes in both Northern Chinese and Cantonese cuisine and are well known for their preparation of seafood in both traditional and exotic styles. Freshly made Hong Kong Style Dim Sum is served daily at lunch.

Daily: lunch 11am-2:30pm, dinner 5pm-10:30pm • 604-682-8833
- 1166 Alberni St. (downtown)
- One of four locations.
- www.kirinrestaurant.com

Le Gavroche

Over the years Le Gavroche has consistently been honored with awards for being the most romantic restaurant, having the most extensive wine list, serving the best French cuisine and providing the most intimate atmosphere in Vancouver. Established in 1979, Le Gavroche is set in a refurbished two-storey Victorian house with a fireplace, an upstairs terrace and sweeping views of Vancouver's Coastal Mountains and harbour. With a private dining room on the main floor, Le Gavroche can accommodate private parties. An avant garde twist to classic French cuisine combined with simple but sensuous sauces, the lightest natural stocks and uncommon aromatic herbs, provide a dining experience like no other.

Dinner daily 5-11pm • 604-685-3924 • 1616 Alberni Street
- www.legavroche.com

Liliget Feast House

Customers entering Liliget arrive in a unique setting, designed by Canada's leading architect Arthur Erickson. An impressive collection of aboriginal art on the walls, furnishings of cedar tables and heavy posts with dimmed lighting, create an atmosphere reminiscent of a Northwest Coast Longhouse. The menu features traditional Northwest Coast Native cuisine with a contemporary edge: The Potlatch Platter, Barbequed Salmon, Oysters, Prawns, Venison, Wild Rice, and Steamed Ferns. Entrées are served in traditional long wooden bowls made from carved cedar and alder. Open daily for dinner, Liliget also offers full service catering.

Summer daily 5-10pm, Winter (Oct.1-Feb.28) Wed-Sun 5-10pm
- 604-681-7044 • 1724 Davie Street • www.liliget.com

Simply Thai Restaurant

Situated in the heart of the trendy Yaletown is Simply Thai Restaurant. It was among the first to prove that Thai food outside Thailand can be absolutely authentic. Along with its evocative flavours of lemon grass, sweet basil and coconut milk, Thai food is the subtle blend of herbs and spices (many imported directly from Thailand) with the crisp freshness of stir-fried vegetables, curries and rich sauces. Chef/Owner Siriwan (Grace) Rerksuttisiridach creates an extraordinary array of distinctive dishes, from pleasantly mild to intensely spicy. Born and raised in Bangkok, she apprenticed with Royal Thai Chefs, whom she goes to see in Thailand every year for further training.

Mon-Fri 11:30-2:30, Mon-Sat 5-10pm
- 604-642-0123
- 1211 Hamilton Street
- www.simplythairestaurant.com

Quattro on Fourth

Located in the heart of Kitsilano, Quattro embraces the senses with a dazzling array of colour and texture. The restaurant offers large round tables for friendly gatherings as well as secluded nooks for romantic evenings. During summer months the lush garden patio is a Vancouver favourite. At the heart of the Quattro experience is the exceptional cuisine from central Italy prepared by chef, Bradford Ellis. Menu highlights are the antipasto platter made for sharing, Pistachio Crusted Sea Bass, Marinated Bocconcini wrapped in Prosciutto and Radiccio, served with Cherry Vinaigrette, and the Spaghetti Quattro.

Sun-Thur 5-10pm, Fri-Sat 5-11pm
- 604-734-4444 • 2611 West Fourth Ave. •
www.quattrorestaurants.com

The Cannery Seafood House

Now entering its 33rd year, The Cannery is one of Vancouver's dining landmarks. Located on the waterfront and specializing in fresh seafood, The Cannery's picturesque setting overlooking the harbour and the North Shore mountains assures guests of a memorable evening. A winner of numerous awards including *Vancouver Magazine's* "Best Seafood Restaurant", and the prestigious "Best of Award of Excellence" from *Wine Spectator* confirms The Cannery Seafood Restaurant as Vancouver's premiere seafood restaurant. Executive Chef Frederic Couton, trained in French and Continental techniques has combined the Pacific Northwest's outstanding fresh ingredients with his global influences to create The Cannery's award-winning menus.

Mon-Fri 11:30-2:30, 5:30-9:30 except holidays, Sat 5-10, Sun 5-9:30.
- 604-254-9606
- 2205 Commissioner Street
- www.canneryseafood.com

The Beach House

The Beach House at Dundarave Pier resides in a lovingly restored designated heritage building, originally built in 1912 overlooking Burrard Inlet. You can wine and dine with an ocean view from the large heated patio on sunny afternoons or moonlit evenings. Executive Chef Robert Byford's new menu reflects the waterfront location with creative fresh fish and shellfish dishes. The wine list is progressive with a smart selection of both Old and New World wines.

Lunch Mon-Sat. 11:30-3pm, dinner Mon-Thur 5-11pm, Fri-Sat 5-12pm, Sunday 5-10pm, Sunday brunch 10:30am • 604-922-1414
- 150-25th Street, West Vancouver
- www.beachhousewestvan.com

The Mill Marine Bistro

The Mill is a European style waterfront bistro located on the Coal Harbour waterfront, overlooking Stanley Park, the North Shore mountains, the seawall and the Georgia Strait. This particular stretch of Coal Harbour is steeped in history with an industrial past. The site of the Mill Marine Bistro was originally home to Vancouver's first mill, Boeing's first seaplane factory and shortly thereafter, CP Rail built their rail station a block away. They are also Vancouver's first and only boat-through. You can either call in your order in advance or right from our 350-foot dock and have it delivered to your boat.

Open Sun-Thur 11am-11pm, Fri-Sat 11am-midnight • 687-MILL (6455)
- 1199 West Cordova Street
- www.millbistro.ca

Rubina Tandoori

Established 20 years ago, Rubina Tandoori is Canada's first HeartSmart Indian Restaurant. It is a family run operation where renowned Krishna Jamal has been the executive chef from the beginning. Her menus have imagination, tradition, style and an abundance of exotic and familiar flavours. Some of the recipes are gathered into a collection: *Krishna Jamal's HeartSmart Flavours of India.* Basic Indian ingredients are wholesome and delicious, with extensive use of fruits and vegetables, whole grains, legumes and dairy products. The food at Rubina is cooked to order and the limited wine list has been chosen specially to complement the dishes. The restaurant is well known for the Green Bottle Masala Curry Lamb Shank, Kashmiri Chili Chicken, Garlic Naan and many other traditional dishes.

Mon-Sat. 5:30-11:pm • 604-874-3621 • 1962 Kingsway Avenue
- www.rubina.com

Gotham Steakhouse and Cocktail Bar

Gotham Steakhouse and Cocktail Bar is the place to go in Vancouver for tender steaks and stiff drinks. This high-end, American-style steakhouse offers a stunningly beautiful dining room, lovely private rooms and one of the city's most urban patios. Executive Chef Bala Kumanan has worked in some of the city's finest kitchens, and now combines his talents with the use of the finest prime beef to produce a simple menu with exquisite ingredients. Be prepared for perfection whether you order something from the fine seafood selection or stay with the traditional. To see a virtual tour of the restaurant visit the web site — www.gothamsteakhouse.com — and follow the links. While you are there, check out the wine list, the menu and get acquainted with the staff. Large parties welcome.

Cocktail Bar, Mon-Fri, 4:00pm-close, Sat, Sun & Holidays, 5:00pm to close Dinner nightly from 5:00pm
- 604-605-8282
- 615 Seymour Street

Banana Leaf Malaysian Restaurant

Banana Leaf Malaysian Restaurant, the award winning restaurant with two locations in Vancouver, is a dining experience not to be missed by anyone who loves Malaysian cuisine. The restaurant offers authentic food from the crossroads of Asia — cuisines from Chinese to East Indian, Thai to Singaporian and Indonesian. Recommended by *Vancouver Magazine, Zagat, Georgia Straight* and many other critics, the Banana Leaf has grown in reputation since opening. A creative approach is taken which has the customer matching ingredients — an abundance of seafood, meat and vegetables — with sauces that are richly flavourful. The restaurant is filled with the aromas of spices, curry and coconut. The food is flavourful and those seeking traditional Malaysian dishes will not be disappointed.

820 West Broadway
Mon-Fri, lunch 11:30am-2:30pm, Sat & Sun, lunch noon-3:00pm
Dinner 7 days a week, 5:00pm-10:00pm • 604-731-6333

1096 Denman Street
Mon through Sun, opens 11:30am.
Sun-Wed, 11:30am-10:00pm, Thurs-Sun, 11:30am-11:00pm
- 604-683-3333

Bin 942 Restaurant

Chef/Owner Gordon Martin created Bin 942 and Bin 941 to reflect New York-styled wine and tapas bars, uniquely designed for Vancouver. Watch the world go by South Granville, sipping on one of the many choices of wines by the glass or enjoying one of Vancouver's finest micro-brewed malt ales. Signature "Tapatisers" such as grilled Nicola Valley Venison, soy-glazed Wentzel Duck Breast or Pan-kissed Sashimi grade Ahi Tuna. Featuring hot music and funky décor the Bins are "...where the hip and gastronomically initiated take their tongues for a good wag..."

Sun, 5:00pm-12:00am,
Mon-Sat, 5:00pm-2:00am
- 604-734-9421
- 1521 West Broadway

The Fish House in Stanley Park

This restaurant is an oasis in the city, where Stanley Park greets English Bay. Enjoy a romantic dinner for two on the patio and taste rare and unusual vintage wines from the private wine cellar. Or enjoy a seasonal celebration, a company party or a wedding. Few restaurants in Vancouver offer award-winning cuisine in the midst of such a beautiful natural setting. Executive Chef Karen Barnaby presides over the kitchen at the Fish House in Stanley Park. Author of *Pacific Passions, Screamingly Good Food* and *The Girls Who Dish*, Karen has a natural, uncomplicated approach to cooking. Sample the restaurant's selection of micro-brewed beers, award-winning wine list and great martinis. Try some of Karen's signature dishes: Ahi Tuna Steak "Diane", Peerless Chocolate Lava Cake and Maple Glazed Salmon.

Mon-Sat lunch from 11:30am
7 days a week dinner from 5:00pm
Sunday Brunch from 11:00am
Afternoon Tea, 7 days a week from 2:00pm-4:00pm • 604-681-7275
or 1-877-681-7275
- 8901 Stanley Park Drive
- info@fishhousestanleypark.com

Feenie's Vancouver

In summer 2003 Chef Rob Feenie opened his new restaurant, Feenie's. A restaurant of casual elegance, approachable dining and exquisite Canadian ingredients all combine to offer a pleasureable dining experience. Open for lunch, brunch and dinner, Feenie's offers a private room, as well as a stylish, comfortable interior. "All Canadian" is *de rigeur* at Feenie's with

affordable wine lists featuring Canadian wines, and other regional specialties from across the country.
Mon-Fri for lunch, Sat & Sun Brunch, All Day bar menu
Dinner 7 nights a week
• 604-739-7115 • 2563 West Broadway • www.lumiere.ca

Lumière Restaurant

Lumière is one of Vancouver's most renowned dining rooms. Star chef, Rob Feenie has put his restaurant and himself on the map by providing his loyal and devout clientele with a truly contemporary Canadian blend of European elegance, North American flair and Asian minimalism. For this young Canadian chef, the simplest cuisine is the most complex. "I hope my food speaks the French I love, the Japanese and Chinese I hear around me in Vancouver and the Canadian I am." Since it opened in 1995, the Lumière Restaurant and Chef Robert Feenie have received accolades from notable food critics around the world. Lumière has been awarded "Vancouver's Best Restaurant" and "Best French Restaurant" awards for an unprecedented six years in a row. In November 2000, Lumière became the first free-standing restaurant in Canada to receive the Relais Gourmand designation. Lumière menus are made up of four, 9-12 course menus. Samplings from the dining room are available in the Tasting Bar, which also offers a more casual *a la carte* menu. Reservations are recommended.

7 days a week, Dinner from 5:30 p.m.
• 604-739-8185 • 2551 West Broadway • www.lumiere.ca
• lumiere@relaischateaux.com

Piccolo Mondo

Winner of numerous awards over many consecutive years for their food and wine list, Piccolo Mondo is the remarkably creative restaurant of Michèle Géris, her husband George Baugh and chef Stéphane Meyer. Passion is what it's all about; passion for food, for Italian wine, for service, and for details. The team makes excellence an everyday achievement thereby fostering longstanding loyalty in their clientele. The restaurant features a small, intimate and elegant dining room that is quiet, refined and formal yet relaxed. "The fish soup alone is worth the journey" said one critic, "but the Salt Cod Brandade is why you'll stay". Stéphane Meyer is a French trained chef who blends his culinary heritage with a northern Italian cuisine, a perfect combination for Vancouver's coastal location and its international population. Reservations recommended.

Mon-Fri, 12:00pm-2:00pm, Mon-Sat, 6:00pm-10:00pm, Closed Sun and statutory holidays. • 604-688-1633
• 850 Thurlow Street
• www.piccolomondoristorante.com

Baru Latino Restaurant

Three young Colombians — two architects and a former anthropologist, who came to Canada in search of a new lifestyle, have created a piece of South America here in Vancouver. Blending new flavours, music and culture, Baru Latino is a comfortable, stylish space where the passion for food and design come together. Flavours from Brazil, Peru, Ecuador, Columbia and Argentina are combined in creative ways for appreciative diners who want to be apart of something new and exciting. This is one of the small culinary wonders of Vancouver, not to be missed for a fun evening out or a late-night sortie. Reservations are accepted until 6:30pm and after that it is on a first come first served basis.

7 days a week, 5:00pm-late, Sat-Sun brunch, 10:00am-2:00pm
• 604-222-9171
• 2535 Alma Street

The Teahouse Restaurant in Stanley Park at Ferguson Point

The Teahouse Restaurant was originally built as a garrison and officer's mess during the Second World War when Ferguson Point was a military installation. It is situated along the scenic shore drive of Stanley Park. In 1994 "Vancouver's Best Patio" was added over-looking English Bay with a breathtaking view. The Teahouse, known as the best place to see the longest sunsets in Vancouver, is open year-round for lunch, dinner and weekend brunch. The Teahouse features local and imported organically grown ingredients. Some of the highlight dishes are the famous Teahouse Stuffed Mushrooms, Organic Carrot Soup, and, because Vancouver is the salmon capital of the world, a special salmon dish is created everyday and is always a winner. The Teahouse is Vancouver's best-kept secret, away from the everyday hustle and bustle of the city.

7 days a week, 11:30am-10:00pm
Sun, brunch, 10:30am-2:30pm
- 604-669-3281 • Ferguson Point, Stanley Park
- www.sequoiarestaurants.com

Blue Water Café

The historic and hip Yaletown neighborhood is home to the Blue Water Cafe — Vancouver's definitive destination for the freshest and best wild seafood. Esteemed Executive Chef James Walt, who has twice cooked at the prestigious James Beard House in New York City, is known for his innovative cuisine that specializes in local, line-caught seafood dishes. Named by Conde Nast Traveler as "one of the world's most exciting new restaurants" Blue Water is housed in a 100-year-old brick and beam heritage warehouse conversion. The dining room offers action views of the open kitchen and raw bar. The main bar leads on to the sunny, heated patio and the private wine cellar (available for parties of up to 28) features thousands of bottles from Blue Water's award-winning wine, sake and bubble selection.

Opens daily 11:30am for lunch, weekend brunch, drinks and dinner.
- 604-688-8078
- 1095 Hamilton Street
- www.bluewatercafe.net

The Observatory

A remarkable confluence of local flavours and worldly techniques gives BC cuisine its unique character. The observatory's contemporary regional menu is dedicated to using the finest ingredients the province has to offer while preserving the integrity of the environment through sustainable practices. Experience the ultimate in fine dining 3700 feet above the glimmering lights of Vancouver. Skyride tickets are complimentary with advance reservations. Fifteen minutes from downtown, the Skyride is open from 9:00am to 10:00pm every day. Reservations for dinner at The Observatory are available on the half hour between 5:00pm and 10:00pm nightly.

Dinner 5:00pm-10:00pm
- 604-998-4403
- 6400 Nancy Greene Way

Wild Rice

Wild Rice is a stylish, trendy restaurant which specializes in modern Chinese cuisine. Designed by Terri Storey, the restaurant is pleasant, inviting and comfortable. Chef Stuart Irving, the man behind the menu, personifies the Zen of cooking. Tom Poirier and Andrew Wong are the partners behind Wild Rice and combined they have over 50 years of experience behind them. Together they make up the team and their enthusiasm is evident in every aspect of the restaurant.

Mon-Fri, lunch 11:30am-4:00pm,
dinner 4:00pm-1:00am, Sat & Sun,
dinner 5:00pm-1:00am
- 604-642-2882
- 117 West Pender Street
- www.wildricevancouver.com

Tojo's Restaurant

Multiple award winning Tojo's is
Vancouver's preferred restaurant for
Japanese food. Opened in 1988,
Hidekazu Tojo is the executive chef,
owner and creative force in this
singular restaurant. Tojo creates a
unique menu. While rooted in tradition
the menu creatively introduces new
food combinations with style and flair,
sure to satisfy both loyal and new
clientele. Tojo's uses only the finest
ingredients, insisting on organic
produce and the highest quality
seafood. Located on the second floor
of a large office tower, Tojo's has
great views of the city and the
mountains. Reservations, which can be
made on-line, are recommended; even
more so if you want to enjoy your meal
in a tatami room.

Mon-Sat, 5pm-midnight.
- 604 872 8050 • 777 West
Broadway • www.tojos.com

Pastis

Pastis has been the winner of
Vancouver Magazine's Best Bistro
award in 1999, 2000 and 2001 and
that's just the start of many awards
this Bistro has received over the years.
Pastis is named after a French licorice
liqueur which is served to whet the
appetite. No one will have to worry
about that here, however, as Pastis
prepares French classic recipes with
contemporary flair that are mouth
watering and delicious. The fine
cuisine along with the largest by-the-
glass wine list in the city (including a
large selection of Pastis) and an ever-
changing taster menu make for a
fabulous meal. Add a warm fireplace,
the ambiance of a Parisian Bistro, the

French maitre d', and you have all the
ingredients for a romantic and
memorable evening. You are now as
close to Paris as you can get without a
plane ticket!

Mon-Sun, 5:30pm-10:30pm.
- 604-731-5020 • 2153 West
4th Avenue • www.pastis.ca

Bishop's

Bishop's is famous for its award
winning, contemporary North
American cuisine. John Bishop and his
executive chef, Dennis Green, have
created a menu and an ambiance like
no other in Vancouver. Every surface
sparkles and every detail has been
thoroughly considered in this most
elegant of dining rooms. Small,
intimate and personal, Bishop's will
not disappoint you. Using only the
finest local ingredients, Dennis Green's
creative take on West Coast Cuisine
delights the taste buds as much as the
eye. Situated in lovely Kitsalano, the
wine list is extensive and the menu
never predictable. Reservations
recommended.

Dinner 7 days a week, 5:30 until
closing • 604-738-2025
- 2183 West 4th Avenue
- www.bishopsonline.com

A Kettle of Fish

The quintessential Vancouver food
experience is found at A Kettle of Fish.
From its opening day in 1979, "the
kettle" as it's affectionately known to
Vancouverites, has been one of
Canada's most acclaimed seafood
restaurants. From B.C. Salmon to Nova
Scotia lobster to Mahi Mahi from the
sunny waters surrounding Hawaii,
every seafood item on the menu is
guaranteed fresh. Always prepared
with passion by Executive Chef
Dobrosav Kovacevic, the seafood
choices on the menu change
seasonally. The kettle's catchy motto is
"eat lotsa fish." Owner Glenn

Anderson's passion for excellence is evident in every aspect of the restaurant. Today his sons Todd and Riley Anderson follow in his footsteps, adding their own personal touches. A Kettle of Fish has a pleasant ambience and is an easy walk from downtown. *En Route Magazine* has repeatedly rated A Kettle of Fish among the best restaurants in the country. Email for reservations.

Dinner, 7 days a week from 5:30pm • 604-682-6661 • 900 Pacific Street (at Hornby) • kettle@telus.net

Akbar's Own Dining Lounge

For a taste of traditional East Indian cuisine at a Vancouver landmark restaurant visit Akbar's Own Dining Lounge. Sample house specialties such as BBQ Eggplant sautéed with onions and tomatoes or the famous Chicken Korma — cooked with raisins, almonds, a dash of butter and light cream. Mint lamb, rolled in spices, and other delicious items from the menu are roasted in the Tandoori oven. Enjoy a fine dining experience in this restaurant that features beautiful Indian tapestries and paintings, creating a warm atmosphere.

Mon-Fri, lunch (except holidays) 11:30am-1:30pm, Dinner, Mon-Sat, 5:00pm-10:00pm, Closed Sundays
• 604-736-8180
• 1905 West Broadway

Rocky Mountaineer Railtours

Billed as "the most spectacular train trip in the world", the tracks were created over a century ago in the Rocky Mountains. A road of steel was laid down which opened up the Canadian West through some of the most rugged terrain in the world. Whether travelling for 2 days or 20, the menu of Executive Chef Mark Jorundson features local produce from the western provinces and harnesses all his creative experience into creating fabulous dining experiences for his guests.

1-800-665-7245 • www.Rockymountaineerrailtours.com

Delilah's

Famous for it's martini's, funky ambience and fabulous interior, Delilah's has long been a Vancouver favourite. Under the stewardship of Chef Jonathon Thauberger, it has one of the tastiest menus and is sure to provide a relaxing and satisfying dining experience. Enjoy the contemporary menu, sip a great martini and enjoy the romance of the evening.

7 days a week, 5:30 until closing • 1789 Comox Street • 604-687-3424

About the Editors

Myriam Leighton is a published writer who co-authored the original book in this series. She is an avid gardener and naturalist who like her co-author, Jennifer Stead, loves to experiment and be creative in her kitchen. Jennifer Stead is a professional artist and educator who gardens and cooks with pleasure. Jennifer and Myriam have co-edited two other books in this series: *Dining Out at Home, Calgary*, and *Dining Out at Home, Edmonton*.

Index

Desserts and Drinks